Thomas Softley Ware

Ware, Thomas S. Hardy Perennials 1893

Thomas Softley Ware

Ware, Thomas S. Hardy Perennials 1893

ISBN/EAN: 9783744763301

Printed in Europe, USA, Canada, Australia, Japan

Cover: Foto ©Andreas Hilbeck / pixelio.de

More available books at **www.hansebooks.com**

ENT. STA. HALL.

Thomas S. Ware

FOUNDER OF THE HALE FARM NURSERIES, 1860.

Telegraphic Address:
"WARE, TOTTENHAM."

A CATALOGUE OF

Hardy Perennials

AND OTHER PLANTS.

No.
143.

....

Spring,

1893.

....

THOS. S. WARE,

Hale Farm Nurseries,

TOTTENHAM, LONDON.

The Nurseries

Adjoin the Tottenham (Hale) Station of the Great Eastern Railway, Cambridge Main Line, to which trains run at frequent intervals from Liverpool Street, the Terminus of the Great Eastern. Trains also run every fifteen minutes from Liverpool Street and Bishopsgate to Seven Sisters Station, which is within ten minutes' walk of the Nurseries. Passengers can book from all parts of the Metropolitan system to either Tottenham (Hale) or Seven Sisters Station. A few trains run daily from St. Pancras to Tottenham (Hale) Station.

To drive from the West End, the best route is by the way of Park Lane, Regent's Park, "York and Albany," "Mother Red Cap," "Brecknock," across Holloway Road by Finsbury Park and "Manor House," and then crossing the High Road, Tottenham, by the "Seven Sisters" Trees, the Nursery will be reached in five minutes.

TERMS.—*Accounts are made up quarterly.* Five per cent. discount *is allowed on amounts of £1 and upwards for cash within one month from each quarter day. For* cash payments *with order, or on receipt of invoice,* 7½ per cent. discount *is allowed on all amounts over £1. A remittance or reference requested from unknown correspondents.*

IN REMITTING *prior to receipt of invoice, my patrons are requested to make an allowance for packing which is as moderate as careful packing will allow.*

POST OFFICE ORDERS *payable at Tottenham,* High Cross. *Small amounts may be remitted in postage stamps.*

COMPLAINTS.—*No complaint can be entertained unless made immediately on receipt of goods.*

RETURNED EMPTIES *usually suffer so much during transit, that when they reach me they are useless, hence all packing material is charged as low as possible consistent with good and careful packing, and* cannot be Allowed for if Returned.

PLANTS *are added gratuitously to reduce the expense of distant carriage and packing.*

INSTRUCTIONS FOR FORWARDING.—*It is requested that the address be written in full, and every information given as to the best mode of forwarding packages.*

ADVICE OF DISPATCH.—*All goods are advised the day of dispatch, and an invoice follows a post or so later.*

CARRIAGE FREE TO LONDON.—*All goods are delivered by my own vans to the Railway Depots in London, excepting such as are for the Cambridge and Norwich portion of the Great Eastern, which are put on rail at Tottenham.*

To my Patrons.

Another year has passed since I last thanked you for your ever increasing support, and the past year has been a still greater success, for which I now ask you to accept my most hearty thanks, and trust I may still receive your continued support, assuring you that everything shall be done to give the utmost satisfaction to all who favour me with their commands.

The past season has been a most unfavourable one; a late cold spring, sudden climatic changes, droughts in some districts and continued rain in others, and in many places severe early frosts, which has caused many families to turn out very unsatisfactorily. In September a very severe frost occurred in the neighbourhood of London, destroying the Dahlias, Chrysanthemums, and many other families, while in some districts they were uninjured until November. I am also afraid that great losses will be experienced owing to the severe weather of December and January, especially to those that were not well established; however, we must hope for a fine spring, which will partially counterbalance the effects of the severity of the weather. In handing you my

143rd Catalogue,

I trust you will find it an improvement upon the last, and a useful guide for the embellishment of your garden. There are many first-class novelties offered and the best of the old varieties, and such as have stood the test of years and are acknowledged to be indispensable in every garden; collections for various soils and situations, and very careful selections made for those who do not know hardy plants, and the Catalogue taken as a whole must be considered a first-class guide as to what to grow and where to grow hardy plants that are adapted for our fickle climate. Everything has been done to make it useful, and the numerous illustrations and descriptions will, in many cases, convey a capital idea of their beauty, and I trust my endeavours will meet with your approval.

Tottenham, February, 1893.   *Thomas S. Ware.*

A

PRIZES AND EXTRACTS FROM PRESS.

I have been awarded First Prize for every Group of Hardy Perennials exhibited by me at the London Shows during the past season.

INTERNATIONAL HORTICULTURAL EXHIBITION, May 27th & 28th, 1892.

FIRST PRIZE for GROUP of HARDY PERENNIALS.

FIRST PRIZE for GROUP of HARDY FLOWERING SHRUBS.

FIRST PRIZE for HARDY PERENNIALS.

Daily Chronicle, May 28th.—"Mr. T. S. Ware won First Prizes for Group of Hardy Flowering Plants; also for Group of Hardy Deciduous Shrubs."

The Garden, International Horticultural Exhibition, May 27th and 28th.—"Mr. Ware was awarded First Prize for an extensive Group of Hardy Deciduous Shrubs in flower, showing chiefly Tree Pæonies, Azaleas, both in great variety, with the new Genista Andreana and Hydrangea, in great variety. Mr. Ware also exhibited a large collection of late Tulips and other things in season, forming a grand group."

ROYAL BOTANIC GARDENS, Regent's Park.

FIRST PRIZE for BULBOUS PLANTS, March 23rd, 1892.

SILVER MEDAL for GROUP of NARCISSUS in pots, March 23rd, 1892.

SILVER MEDAL for GROUP of PRIMULAS, &c., April 27th, 1892.

FIRST PRIZE for HARDY PERENNIALS in pots, May 18th, 1892.

SILVER MEDAL for TREE PÆONIES, May 18th, 1892.

Daily News, March 24th.—"For Narcissus, Mr. Ware, of Tottenham, maintained his pride of place."

Daily Telegraph, May 19th.—"Mr. T. S. Ware's Tree Pæonies were the centre of attraction."

Bell's Weekly Messenger and Farmers' Journal, May 19th.—"Mr. T. S. Ware exhibited some beautiful Primulas, Daffodils, North American Orchids, &c., &c., which made a very pretty group."

Gardeners' Chronicle, May 21st.—"For a Collection of Hardy Herbaceous Plants Mr. Ware was First; also exhibited a fine Collection of Tree Pæonies, &c., &c."

The Garden, May 21st.—"Mr. T. S. Ware had the best Collection of Hardy Plants in pots, a Silver Medal for a large Collection of Pæonies; also, a small Silver Medal for a Collection of Tulips."

Journal of Horticulture.—"The miscellaneous exhibits were as usual remarkably fine. Mr. Ware had a splendid group of Tree Pæonies and Azalias in the large Marquee, for which he was deservedly awarded a Silver Medal, and in the Corridor he had a brilliant Collection of Hardy Cut Flowers, among which were 100 varieties of Darwin Tulips of most remarkable colours."

ROYAL HORTICULTURAL SOCIETY, Temple Show, May 25th & 26th, 1892.

SILVER-GILT FLORA MEDAL for PÆONIES and CUT FLOWERS.

SILVER-GILT FLORA MEDAL for BEGONIAS.

SILVER BANKSIAN MEDAL for GROUP of CARNATIONS, August 9th, 1892.

SILVER BANKSIAN MEDAL for NARCISSUS, &c., MARCH 8th, 1892.

Journal of Horticulture, May 26th.—"A fine display of Begonias was also made by Mr. T. S. Ware; also, a fine group of Tree Pæonies."

Gardening World, May 28th.—"Mr. T. S. Ware follows on with a striking group of Tree Pæonies; also, well to the front with Begonias."

Gardeners' Magazine, May 28th.—Hardy Flowers, au extensive display came from Mr. T. S. Ware; also, a charming group of Begonias."

ROYAL CALEDONIAN SOCIETY, September, 1892.
AWARDED SEVEN FIRST-CLASS CERTIFICATES for NEW BEGONIAS.
GLASGOW HORTICULTURAL SOCIETY, September, 1892.
AWARDED THREE AWARDS of MERIT for NEW BEGONIAS.

Journal of Horticulture. July 12th, 1892, Royal Horticultural Society.—"Hardy Flowers were shown by Mr. T. S. Ware, of Tottenham, the collection including many choice things, such as Achillea The Pearl, Lilies, and many other choice things. Received an Award of Merit for Lilium Bloomerianum Magnificum, and a First-Class Certificate for Calopogan Pulchellus ; and was awarded a Silver Banksian Medal."

The Garden. May 18th, Royal Botanic Society.—"Mr. T. S. Ware, Tottenham, had the best collection of Hardy Plants in Pots Staging . . . . and was awarded First Prize."

Daily Chronicle, May 26th.—"Mr. Ware, of Tottenham, displayed an excellent Collection of Tree Pæonies from Japan."

Daily News, May 26th.—"Mr. Ware took Silver-gilt Medals for Pæonies, Cut-flowers, and Miscellaneous plants."

Journal of Horticulture. September 2nd and 3rd, Crystal Palace.—"Mr. T. S. Ware contributed a very extensive group of Dahlias, comprising all the very finest kinds in cultivation."

INTERNATIONAL HORTICULTURAL EXHIBITION, Earl's Court, July 5th & 6th, 1892.
FIRST PRIZE for a GROUP of BEGONIAS, occupying a space of 150 square feet.
FIRST PRIZE for a GROUP of HARDY PERENNIALS.
SILVER MEDAL for a COLLECTION of HARDY FLOWERS.
SEVEN FIRST CLASS CERTIFICATES for NEW PLANTS.
SILVER MEDAL for BEGONIAS, May 27th & 28th, 1892.

Daily Graphic, May 26th.—"Brief mention only can be given to the Begonias and Pæonies of Mr. T. S. Ware, which were simply superb."

Morning Advertiser, May 26th.—"Equally striking was the bank of Japanese Pæonies belonging to Mr. T. S. Ware ; also, an extensive stand of Begonias."

Journal of Horticulture, August 9th, 1892.—"Mr. T. S. Ware, of Tottenham, exhibited a Collection of Carnations in bunches, with their own foliage, which were extremely attractive and showing the effectiveness of these charming flowers for cutting. A Silver Banksian Medal was awarded."

Fashionable London, May 28th.—"Mr. T. S. Ware's collections of Tree Pæonies, Tulips, and Primulas were unrivalled, and were surrounded by crowds of admirers."

Bell's Weekly Messenger and Farmers' Journal. June 6th.—"T. S. Ware also showed some good Begonias, and a large collection of Tree Pæonies, which were very much admired by all visitors."

ROYAL HORTICULTURAL SOCIETY, Drill Hall, Westminster, July 12th.
SILVER MEDAL for a COLLECTION of LILIES.
INTERNATIONAL HORTICULTURAL EXHIBITION, August 1st, 1892.
SILVER MEDAL for GROUP of CARNATIONS and GAILLARDIAS.

Journal of Horticulture.—"Mr. T. S. Ware had a Collection of Border Carnations and Gaillardias of great beauty, and was awarded a Silver Medal."

The Garden. July 5th and 6th, International Horticultural Exhibition.—" The Competition for Cut Herbaceous and Bulbous Perennials produced a good display. In the Trade Class Mr. T. S. Ware staged a grand collection, and was worthily awarded the First Prize."

Financial Truth, July 9th.—"The Collections of Mr. Ware, of Tottenham, were magnificent, his display of Begonias taking the First Prize, and also his show of Hardy and Herbaceous Plants gained a similar honour."

Lady's Pictorial, July 16th.—" The Hardy Herbaceous Plants shown by T. S. Ware, and which secured First Prize, were remarkably fine."

TOTTENHAM COLLECTION
OF
HARDY BORDER PLANTS.

Being a carefully REVISED SELECTION of plants adapted for any garden, containing only FREE GROWING VARIETIES, and the best of their respective families, and such as can be grown in any ordinary border without any special attention, and are QUITE HARDY All are STRONG PLANTS, and the MAJORITY ADAPTED FOR CUTTING PURPOSES, and every plant can be thoroughly recommended.

MANY FIRST PRIZES FOR HARDY PERENNIALS DURING 1892.

Achillea mongolica, 1/-
—— Ptarmica fl. pl., 6d., 9d.
—— serrata fl. pl., 9d. ; 8/- doz.
—— The Pearl, 1/6
Aconitum napellus bicolor, 9d.
Adonis vernalis, 6d.
Agrostemma hybrida, 9d.
—— flos-jovis, 6d. ; 5/- doz.
Alstroemeria chilensis, 6d.
—— psittacina, 6d.
Anemone sulphurea, 1/6 & 2/6
—— japonica, 6d. & 9d.
—— alba, 6d. & 9d.
—— sylvestris, 9d.
Anthericum Liliastrum, 9d.
—— major, 1/-
—— algeriense, 9d.
Aquilegia chrysantha, 9d.
—— coerulea hybrida, 9d.
—— californica hybrida, 9d.
Armeria cephalotes rubra, 9d.
—— plantaginea rubra, 9d.
Aster amellus bessarabicus, 9d.
—— longifolius formosus, 6d.
—— formosissimus, 9d.
Campanula dahurica, 9d.
—— grandis alba, 9d.
—— Hendersoni, 9d. & 1/-
—— persicifolia alba fl. pl.,
            6d. & 9d.
—— —— grandiflora, 1/-
—— Van Houttei pallida, 9d.
Carnations in variety, 6d. to 1/.
Centaurea montana, 3 colours,
   red, white and blue, 6d.
—— dealbata, 9d.
Chelone obliqua, 9d.
Chrysanthemum latifolium,
   9d ; 8/- doz.
—— maximum, 9d.
Coreopsis lanceolata, 6d.
—— grandiflora, 1/6
—— verticillata, 1/-
Corydalis nobilis, 9d. & 1/-
Delphinium, several first-class
   named varieties, 9d. to 1/6
Dictamnus Fraxinella, 9d. & 1/

Dictamnus Fraxinella alba, 1/-
Dielytra formosa, 9d.
Doronicum austriacum, 9d.
—— plantagineum excelsum,
   9d.
Echinops ritro, 9d.
Erigeron aurantiaca, 9d.
—— speciosum superbum, 6d.
Eryngium giganteum, 1/-
Funkia grandiflora, 9d.
—— japonica lutea, 9d.
Gaillardia magnifica, 9d.
—— maxima, 1/-
Gentiana Andrewsi, 1/-
Geum coccineum plenum, 9d.
—— miniatum, 9d.
Gillenia trifoliata, 1/-
Gypsophila paniculata, 6d.
Harpalium rigidum, 9d.
Helianthus multiflorus major
   9d. ; 8/- doz.
—— —— plenus, 9d.
—— —— maximus, 9d.
—— —— Soleil d'or, 9d.
—— laetiflorus, 9d.
Hemerocallis flava, 9d.
—— disticha pl., 9d.
—— fulva, 6d.
—— Dumortieri, 9d.
Helleborus niger maximus, 1/6
—— niger major, 1/-, 1/6 & 2/6
—— punctatissima, 1/6
Hollyhocks, 3 fine double
   vars., all distinct colours, 1/-
Hypericum Moserianum, 1/-
   & 1/6
—— Uralum, 9d.
Hesperis matronalis alba pl.,
   6d.
Inula glandulosa, 1/-
Iris, 3 of the most distinct, 9d.
Lathyrus grandiflorus, 1/-
Liatris spicata, 6d.
Lindelofia longifolia, 1/-
Lychnis chalcedonica plena,
   1/-
—— dioica rubra plena, 9d.

Lychnis viscaria splendens
   plena, 9d.
Lupinus polyphyllus albus, 6d.
Megasea cordifolia purpurea,
   9d.
Monarda didyma, 6d.
Morina longifolia, 9d.
Œnothera speciosa, 9d.
—— Youngi, 9d.
Papaver bracteata, 1/-
—— Prince of Orange, 1/-
—— orientale, 6d.
Pentstemon glaber, 9d.
—— barbatus Torreyi, 6d.
Phlox decussata, 6 of the most
   distinct varieties, 6d. each.
Pink, Clove pink, 9d.
—— Early Blush, 6d.
—— fimbriata alba major, 6d.
Polemonium himalaicum, 9d.
—— Richardsoni, 9d.
Potentillas, 3 double and 3
   single varieties, 9d each.
Pyrethrum hybridum, 3 single
   varieties, 9d. each.
—— 3 double vars., 9d. ea.
Ranunculus aconitifolius
   plenus, 9d.
—— speciosus, 9d.
Rudbeckia Newmanni, 6d.
—— maxima, 1/-
Scabiosa caucasica, 9d.
Senecio Doronicum, 6d.
—— pulcher, 9d. & 1/-
Sidalcea candida, 9d.
Spiraea aruncus, 9d.
—— astilboides, 2/6
—— filipendula plena, 6d. & 9d.
—— palmata alba, 1/-
Statice Gmelina, 9d.
—— latifolia, 9d.
Stokesia cyanea, 9d. & 1/-
Symphytum officinale var. 9d.
Tiarella cordifolia, 6d. & 9d.
Tritoma Burchelli, 1/-
Trollius Loddigesiana, 9d.
Veronica subsessilis, 9d.

100 Plants, my selection from the above, for 55s. ; 50 for 25s.

10 Plants will be sent gratuitously with every order for 100 Plants.

CHEAPER SELECTIONS CAN BE MADE, SEE PAGE 6.

TOTTENHAM COLLECTION
OF
HARDY ROCK PLANTS.

Being a select list of free-growing, hardy, dwarf perennials adapted for the rockery, or for the front row of a border; such varieties as can be grown without any elaborate preparation of the soil in any ordinary border, and increase both in size and beauty annually. All are showy, very free flowering, and quite hardy; these with a * are for a shady border in light soil, the remainder for full sun.

MANY FIRST PRIZES FOR PERENNIALS DURING 1892.

Acantholimon glumaceum, 9d.
Aciphylla Lyalli, 1/6
Androsace carnea, 1/-
—— sarmentosa, 9d.
*Anemone apennina, 6d.
*—— —— alba, 1/-
*—— narcissiflora, 9d.
*—— palmata, 6d.
—— —— alba, 9d.
—— stellata fulgens, 6d.
*—— vernalis, 1,6
Aquilegia glandulosa, true, 9d
Arabis albida fol. var., 6d.
Armeria bracteata rubra, 9d.
Arenaria purpurascens, 9d.
Aster alpinus, 6d. and 9d.
—— —— speciosus, 1·
Aubrietia Campbelli, improved, 6d. ; 5/- doz.
—— Leichtlini, 9d.; 8/- doz.
Calandrinia umbellata, 6d.
Callirhoe involucrata, 6d.
—— lineariloba, 9d.
*Campanula abietina, 9'-
*—— fragilis, 9d.
*—— isophylla alba, 1/-
*—— muralis, 9d.
*—— pumila alba, 6d.
*—— pulla, 9d.
*Cardamine trifoliata, 9d.
Cheiranthus Alpinus, 6d.
*Cyclamen, hederæfolium, 6d.
*—— Atkinsi, in variety, 9d.
*—— repandum, 9d.
Cypripedium spectabile, 1/6 and 2/6
—— Calceolus, 1/-
—— pubescens, 1/6 and 2/6
Delphinium nudicaule, 9d.
Dianthus Cœsius, 6d.
Dielytra formosa, 9d.
*Epigæa repens, 2/6
*Epimedium alpinum, 9d.
*—— niveum roseum, 1/-

*Epimedium niveum, 9d.
Erodium Manescavi, 9d.
*Ferns, in 6 vars., 6d. & 9d.
*Gaultheria procumbens, 1/6
Gentiana acaulis, 6d. & 1,-
—— septemfida, 1/-
*—— pneumonanthe, 9d.
Geranium argenteum, 1,6
—— sanguineum, 6d.
Geum montanum, 9d.
Gypsophila prostrata, 6d.
Helianthemum, 6 distinct varieties at 6d.
Heuchera sanguinea, 9d. & 1/-
*Hepatica angulosa, 9d.
*—— single blue, 6d. to 1/6
*—— double red, 6d. to 1/-
Iberis corifolia, 6d.
·—— sempervirens plena, 9d.
Lewisia rediviva, 2/6
*Linaria pallida, 6d.
Linum flavum, 9d.
Lithospermum prostratum, 6d. & 9d.
Lychnis alpina, 6d.
—— flos cuculi alba pl., 1/-
—— Haageana, 6d.
*Myosotis elegantissima, 6d.
*Nierembergia rivularis, 1/-
*Œnothera macrocarpa, 6d.
*—— riparia, 9d.
*Ourisia coccinea, 1/-
Oxalis floribunda rosea, 6d.
Papaver nudicaule alba, 6d.
—— —— miniatum, 6d.
Pentstemon heterophyllus, 9d. ; 8/- doz.
Phlox amœna, 9d. ; 8/- doz.
—— Canadensis alba, 1/-
—— procumbens, 9d.
—— setacea atropurpurea, 6d.
—— —— Bride, 9d.
*Primula japonica, 9d. ; 8/- dz.
—— farinosa, 6d.
—— Clusiana, 1/6

*Primula auricula, 9d.
—— glaucescens, 1,6
—— integrifolia, 9d.
—— longifolia, 9d.
*—— marginata, 1,6
*—— rosea, 9d. ; 8/- doz.
*—— Rusbyi, 2,6
*—— Sieboldi, several varieties, 9d. to 1/-
—— viscosa, 9d.
*—— nivalis, 1/-
*Ramondia pyrenaica, 9d & 1/
*Ranunculus amplexicaulis, 6d. & 9d.
*Rhexia virginica, 1/-
Saxifraga Burseriana, 1,6 and 2/6
*—— Camposi, 6d.
—— Hosti, 9d.
—— lantoscana superba, 1/, 1/6
—— longifolia, 1/- & 1/6
—— pyramidalis, 9d.
—— sancta, 1/-
Scabiosa graminifolia, 9d.
Sedum, 4 distinct varieties, 6d.
Sempervivum, 4 vars. at 6d.
Silene acaulis alba, 6d.
—— maritima fl. pl., 9d.
—— Schaftæ, 9d.
*Sisyrinchium grandiflorum, 9d. ; 8/- doz.
Soldanella alpina, 9d.
*Thalictrum anemonoides, 9d
—— adiantifolium, 9d.
Thymus montanus albus, 6d.
—— lanuginosus, 6d.
*Trillium grandiflorum, 9d.
*Tussilago alpina, 6d.
Veronica incana, 6d.
—— repens, 6d.
—— rupestris, 6d.
*Viola pedata, 1/-
*—— —— bicolor, 1/-
Zauschneria californica, 9d.
—— splendens, 9d.

100 Plants, my selection from above, for 55s. ; 50 for 25s. and 30s.
10 Plants will be sent gratuitously with every order for 100 plants.
CHEAPER COLLECTIONS CAN BE MADE, SEE PAGE 6.

Selections of Hardy Perennials.

The following selections will be found very useful to those who have not a thorough knowledge of this class of plants. The selections will contain nothing but really first-class varieties entirely of my selection, and such as are adapted for the various situations; all will be good plants, true to name, and such as I feel sure will please.

No. 1.   Selections of Rock Plants.

For growing in hot situations on the rockwork, old walls, ruins, &c. Also for moist shady positions on the rockery.

12 varieties for.........5s., 6s. 6d., 8s., 10s. & 12s.	50 varieties for ....26s., 32s. to 60s.
25 ,, ,, ...10s. 6d., 13s., 16s., 20s. & 25s.	100 ,, ,, ... 40s., 50s., 60s., 70s. & 80s.

No. 2. Selections of Dwarf Perennials for mixed Borders.

Growing from 6 to 15 inches in height, for the front row of a sunny or shady border.

12 varieties for..............5s., 6s. 6d., 8s. & 10s.	50 varieties for ....18s. 6d., 25s., 35s. & 50s.
25 ,, ,, ...10 6d., 16s. and 20s.	100 ,, ,, ...30s., 50s. & 75s.

No. 3. Selections of Perennials for mixed Borders.

Varying in height from 2 to 4 feet, for sunny or shady positions, flowering at various seasons, so that the border is always gay.

12 varieties for.........5s., 6s. 6d., 8s., 10s. to 18s.	50 varieties for...18s. 6d., 25s., 30s., 40s. & 50s.
25 ,, 8s. 6d., 10s. 6d., 13s., 16s., 20s. to 30s.	100 ,, ,, ... 30s., 40s., 55s., 65s. & 75s.

No. 4.   Selections for Autumn Decoration.

12 varieties for............6s., 8s., 10s., 12s. & 15s.	50 varieties for...............30s., 40s., 50s. to 70s.
25 ,, ,, ... 13s., 16s., 20s., 25s. & 40s.	100 in 50 varieties for ....50s. to 100s.

No. 5.   Selections for Spring Decoration.

Comprising the best of the Spring Flowers, adapted for massing, or for rockwork or border.

12 varieties for ....5s., 6s. 6d., 8s. to 10s	50 varieties for ....21s., 27s. 6d. & 35s.
25 ,, ,, ... 10s. 6d., 13s., 16s. to 20s.	100 in 50 varieties for............40s., 50s. and 75s.

No. 6.   Selections for Growing in Towns.

Composed of such species and varieties as will thrive in smoky atmospheres.

12 varieties for ....5s., 6s. 6d., 8s. to 10s.	50 varieties for...............26s., 32s., 40s. to 60s.
25 ,, ,, ... 10s. 6d., 13s., 16s. to 20s.	100 ,, ,, ... 40s., 50s., 60s. & 75s.

No. 7.   Special Selections for any Situation
Can be made upon application.

10 plants will be sent gratuitously with every order for 100 plants.

A Selection of

HARDY PERENNIALS

AND

ROCK PLANTS.

NOTE.—All these are quite hardy under ordinary circumstances, except those with a (*), and all will thrive in an ordinary border or rockwork, except where stated to the contrary. In all cases where I have seeds to offer, I have quoted price per packet.

Acantholimon glumaceum (*Statice ararati*), a charming little rock plant, forming cushions of dark green, spiny foliage, from which issue numerous one-sided spikes of rose coloured flowers 1½ inches across, 6 to 12 in a spikelet. It will thrive in almost any soil or situation, is perfectly hardy, and one I can highly recommend. 9d. each.

Acanthus Candelabrum. This is an acquisition to our list of hardy ornamental foliage plants. It belongs to a genus of stately growing herbaceous plants, with enormous laciniated foliage, often from 1½ to 3 feet in length. The flowers are reddish and white, and produced in large dense erect spikes, which often attain the height of 4 feet, and is among the most conspicuous objects that a garden can possess. 1s. each.

Acanthus spinosus, large pinnate spiny foliage, of a deep green glossy colour; a bold massive plant. 1s. each.

Acanthus spinosissimus, handsome foliage, covered with white spines; very distinct. 1s. each.

Achillea Clavennæ, compact tufts of hoary foliage, and numerous heads of white flowers; fine as an edging or rock plant. 9d. each.

Achillea Mongolica, a first-class perennial, hardy, very free growing, soon forming large clumps in almost any soil or situation, producing large corymbs of snow-white flowers. As a decorative plant it is one of the very best, and will be held in high esteem for decoration and cutting purposes. 1s. each; 10/6 doz.

Achillea Ptarmica fl. pl., one of the most useful of our border perennials, erect stems 2½ft., terminating with small white flowers, and exceedingly double; for cutting purposes it is invaluable, and as a decorative plant it can be highly recommended. 6d. and 9d.; 5s. and 8s. doz. Seed, 1s. per pkt.

Achillea Ptarmica, "The Pearl." I would specially call your attention to this splendid novelty, as it unquestionably is one of the finest introductions for many years, and will rapidly find a place in every garden, and be grown by acres by the Market Growers. It is a variety of the common double *Sneezewort*, which is known to all as one of the very best perennials in cultivation for cutting purposes. The variety now under consideration is similar in every respect, but having flowers more than double the size, much purer in colour, and produced in such marvellous quantities as to render it an exceptional plant; second to none in my collection, and invaluable for almost any purpose. Was awarded a First-Class Certificate at the International Horticultural Exhibition, Earl's Court, July 5th, 1892. 1s. 6d.; 15s. doz.

Achillea serrata, fl. pl., similar in general appearance to *Ptarmica plena*, but the flowers not so double, but of a purer white, leaves very deeply cut, and blooming later than preceding, and on that account useful for cutting. A first-class perennial. 9d.; 8s. dozen.

Achillea tomentosa, a neat creeping evergreen, with numerous large flat heads of bright yellow flowers on stems 6 inches in height; flowering early in spring, and very useful for cutting, the rockery, massing, &c. 6d.; 5s. dozen.

Aciphylla squarrosa, remarkable New Zealand plant, known in the colony as *Bayonet Plant*, or *Spear Grass*. It forms large circular bushes composed of long tri-pinnate stiff, spiny foliage, densely set together like so many bayonets, and throwing up a centre spike 6 to 9 feet high of white flowers, forming a striking plant on the rockwork or border, preferring dryish soil and a sunny situation. It is found growing in high mountainous regions, where the frost is very severe and snow lays for many weeks. 2/6

Aciphylla Colensoi, another species, quite distinct, and one I can recommend. 1s. each.

Adonis pyrenaica, see page 9.

Aciphylla Lyalli, another species, similar in growth to *A squarrosa*, but with larger leaves edged with brown, flowers white and quite hardy. 1s. 6d. each.

Aconitum, an important genus of perennials, having stout erect stems 2 to 5 feet high, bearing numerous helmet-shaped flowers—blue, yellow, white, and purple. Many of the varieties are exceedingly ornamental, perfectly hardy and easily grown, and should be planted very extensively in herbaceous borders, woodland walks, &c. Seed, mixed, 3d. pkt.

Aconitum anthora, a curious Pyrenean species, growing about 2 feet in height, having large yellow flowers. 9d. each; 8s. doz.

Aconitum autumnale, spikes of large lavender-blue flowers, about 3 feet in height, one of the best of the autumn flowering perennials. 9d. each; 8s. doz.

Aconitum Japonicum, a very rare and beautiful plant, distinct from all of this group. It grows about 2 feet in height, having very large dark green glossy foliage, and stout spikes of deep blue flowers in late autumn. 1s. 6d. each.

Aconitum Ochroleucum. Another very distinct variety having handsome dark green foliage, and spikes of pale yellow flowers. 1s. each.

6 distinct varieties, for 4s. 6d.

Actæa spicata fructo-rubro, an interesting plant, flowers white, in bunches, not effective by any means, but when covered with scarlet berries in autumn is well worth attention. 1s. each.

Adonis pyrenaica, a charming Pyrenean species, unquestionably one of the most distinct and beautiful of all our spring flowers, but unfortunately rare and difficult to obtain. It grows 18 inches in height, forming a thick mass of Fennel-like foliage, and numerous stout stems, each terminating with a large solitary Anemone-like flower, 2½ to 4 inches in diameter, and of the most lovely golden-yellow colour. It might be described as a gigantic form of *Adonis vernalis*, but far more beautiful in every respect, growing freely in any rich loam. *See* Illustration, page 8. 2s. 6d. each ; 24s. doz.

Adonis vernalis, a well known flowering plant, the flowers are bright golden-yellow, Anemone-like, from 2 to 3 inches across, borne in great profusion on short stalks, it is a first-class plant, and one I can thoroughly recommend. 6d. ; 5s. per doz.

*Agapanthus, a showy group for autumn decoration, having ornamental foliage and large umbels of various shades of blue and white flowers. When grown in pots in a cool conservatory they make grand specimens, and last in flower a long time.

Agapanthus Mooreanus, a comparatively new and hardy African species, of great beauty, dwarf habit, with lovely heads of bright blue flowers. 9d. ; 8s. doz.

Agapanthus umbellatus, a grand plant for autumn decoration ; foliage very ornamental, with gigantic umbels of bright blue flowers. 9d. ; 8s. doz.

*Agapanthus umbellatus albus, heads of pure white flowers, very useful for autumn decoration. 1s. each.

*Agapanthus umbellatus maximus, a robust growing variety of the preceding. 1s. ; 10,6 doz.

Allium pedemontanum.

Agrostemma Flos-Jovis, forms a pretty symmetrical bush, about 2 feet in height, having soft dowy foliage, and clustered heads of bright rose-coloured flowers, continuing in blossom for a long time. A first-class plant for cutting. 6d. ; 5s. doz. Seed, 3d. per pkt.

Agrostemma coronaria hybrida, a cross between *A. Flos-Jovis* and *A. Coronaria*, and one of the most beautiful of this invaluable genus, far surpassing either parents in brilliancy of colour and constitutional vigour. It has been in cultivation for several years, but curiously has only found its way into a few hands, but will I am certain become one of our most popular perennials. I may repeat that it is quite distinct in colour, the individual blossoms much larger and in every way decidedly superior to either parent and second to no herbaceous perennial in English gardens, being one of the most welcome hybrids ever raised. Extra strong plants, 9d. ; 8s. doz.

Agrostemma coronaria fl. pl., this is a double variety of the "*Rose Campion*," flowers very double of a rich deep crimson, growing about 2 feet high, easily propagated by division, and remaining in flower for a long time. 1s. ; 10s. 6d. doz.

Aletris farinosa (*American Star Grass*), forming tufts of lance-shaped ribbed foliage, and long spikes of white bell-shaped flowers; a beautiful plant for hot sandy soils; very rare. 1s. 6d. ea.

Allium pedemontanum, the finest of the family, large campanulate flowers of a deep vinous purple, on stems about a foot high. The flowers are of great substance, and, either on the plant, or in a cut state, are of great duration. Was unanimously awarded a First-class Certificate by the Royal Horticultural Society. This is a plant I can strongly recommend either for the Border or Rockery. Strong plants in pots, 1s. ; 10s. 6d. doz. *See* Fig. above.

Alyssum saxatile compactum (*Gold Dust*), a charming spring flowering perennial, admirably adapted for bedding, massing, or rockwork. 4d. each ; 3s. doz. ; 21s. 100. Seed, 3d. per pkt.

Alstrœmeria chilensis.   *Anthericum Liliastrum major* (see page 13)

Alstrœmeria, a lovely group of hardy tuberous-rooted plants, producing flowers of great brilliancy of almost every shade of colour. For cutting they are invaluable; some of the varieties are grown in large quantities for supplying Covent Garden with cut flowers. The following will be sent in pots.

Alstrœmeria aurea, very showy, with bright orange-coloured flowers in umbels, a really first-class cutting plant; quite hardy. In pots, 6d.; 5s. doz. Stronger, 9d.; 8s. doz. Seed, 6d. pkt.

Alstrœmeria chilensis, dwarf-growing species, immense heads of bloom, varying in shades of white, lilac, rose, salmon, &c. 6d. each. Seed, 6d. per packet.

Alstrœmeria psittacina, dark crimson splashed with mahogany. 6d.

*•**Alstrœmeria peregrina,** large heads of purple flowers, beautifully striped. A lovely plant for a warm dry situation; protected during severe weather or grown in pots. 1s. 6d.

*•**Alstrœmeria peregrina alba,** a gem, umbels of snow-white flowers, one of the most beautiful tuberous-rooted plants in my collection, should be grown in a dry sunny situation or in pots; for cutting it is grand. 2s. 6d.

Anchusa italica, a strong growing perennial, covered the whole of the summer with intense Gentian-blue flowers; an invaluable plant for "Bees." 6d. each. Seed, 3d. pkt.

Androsace carnea, one of the most beautiful of our spring flowers; clusters of pink blossoms with a yellow eye, frequently before the snow has disappeared. Good plants, 1s. each.

Androsace helvetica, dense compact tufts similar to a *Saxifraga,* covered with pure white flowers; very scarce, a few only to offer. 2s. 6d. and 3s. 6d. each.

Androsace Leichtlini (*new*), a very distinct variety, producing long trailing stems with white silky foliage, and numerous umbels of white flowers with a conspicuous pink centre, lasting in flower nearly the whole of summer; apparently a very fine variety of *A. lanuginosa.* 2s. 6d.

Androsace sarmentosa, a very interesting species from the Himalayas, forming rosettes of downy foliage, not unlike *Sempervivum arachnoideum.* Flowers in umbels, large, bright rose with white centres. One of the most beautiful of this genus, and very easy to grow, preferring a sandy loam, with the foliage resting on stones to keep it dry. 9d. each.

Androsace villosa, one of the most lovely of the Alpine flora, forming little hillocks of soft silky foliage, totally obscured by a multitude of white flowers, having red or yellow eyes. 2s. 6d. each.

Androsace vitaliana (*Aretia vitaliana*), a showy and vigorous species, covering the ground like a carpet, and producing innumerable yellow flowers, thriving well in loam and grit. 1s. ea.

Anemone alpina, one of the most beautiful of the Alpine flora, and as easily grown as any border plant, growing about 2 feet in height, producing large white flowers of great substance, slightly tinted with blue on the exterior, somewhat resembling a "Pæony," and exceptionally free blooming, very similar in general appearance to *A. Sulphurea* figured on page 11. 1/- & 1/6.

Anemone sulphurea.   *Anemone vernalis (see page 12).*

Anemone alpina sulphurea, by far the handsomest species of this genus, and certainly one of the most beautiful hardy plants in cultivation. The deep lemon or sulphur yellow of the flowers contrast most exquisitely with the foliage. Flourishes freely in any ordinary border, and, when established, one of the foremost of rock or border plants. A beautiful plate appeared in *Garden*, 1889. 1s. 6d.; 15s. doz. Stronger, 2s. 6d.; 24s. doz. *See* Fig.

Anemone apennina, charming masses of brilliant blue flowers, as large as half-a-crown, very early in spring; fine for bedding or naturalizing. Strong, established in pots, 6d.; 5s. doz.

Anemone apennina alba, a white form of the preceding, an uncommon and beautiful variety; established plants, in pots, 1s.; 10s. 6d. doz.

Anemone blanda, the Greek form of *Apennina*, flowers as large as a shilling, varying from light to dark blue. 9d. each.

Anemone blanda atrocœrulea, this is without doubt one of the most charming of this group, intense deep blue flowers as large as a florin, frequently before the snow disappears, very rare. Established in pots, 1s. each; 10s. 6d. doz.

Anemone (coronaria and stellata varieties). *See* my Begonia and Gladiolus Catalogue.

Anemone fulgens, flowers dazzling scarlet, very early. Strong, established plants, 6d.; 5s. doz.

Anemone fulgens grandiflora (*The Greek variety*), this is the most showy of the scarlet group, and one of the most effective of our spring flowers. The blossoms are as large as a half-crown, of a dazzling scarlet, and produced in great abundance. 9d. each; 7s. 6d. doz.

Anemone fulgens multipetala, this is a semi-double variety of *A. Fulgens*, flowers exceedingly brilliant in colour, a first-class plant for cutting in early spring. Plants in pots, 6d.; 5s. doz.

Anemone japonica, a very handsome group of autumn-flowering perennials; these, which are among the most effective of our autumn-blooming plants, are all hardy, easily grown in almost any soil, forming large bushes, smothered with showy white, red and rose-coloured flowers. Plants, 6d. each; 5s. doz. Extra strong, 9d. each; 7s. 6d. doz.

Anemone japonica hybrida, rose coloured flowers. 6d.; 5s. doz. Extra strong, 9d.; 7s. 6d. doz.

Anemone japonica alba (*Honorine Joubert*), one of the best in my collection, and should be in every garden, flowers white. 6d. each; 5s. doz. Strong, 9d.; 7s. 6d. doz. Seed, 1s. 6d. pkt.

Anemone japonica alba (*Lady Ardliaun*), a new variety recently introduced, which I have not yet flowered. 2s. each.

Anemone narcissiflora (*The Narcisse-flowered Wind Flower*), a pretty and interesting plant, bearing umbels of showy white flowers, totally distinct from all others of this family. 9d.

Anemone nemorosa alba plena (*The Double White Wood Anemone*), a beautiful plant for a moist shady situation, forming carpets of lovely light green foliage, and myriads of double white flowers. Strong, 6d. each; 5s. doz.

Anemone nemorosa cœrulea, a sky-blue variety of the *Wood Anemone*, quite distinct from *Robinsoniana*, remarkably free blooming, and in a mass is remarkably effective. 6d.; 5s. doz.

Anemone palmata alba.   *Anemone fulgens.* See page 11.

Anemone nemerosa Robinsoniana, one of the most beautiful of this family, producing in great abundance large sky-blue flowers, on slender stems 9 inches high, the flowers are double the size of the ordinary *Wood Anemone,* and of a most lovely shade. 1s.; 10s. 6d. doz.

Anemone palmata (*Lobata*), (*The Cyclamen-leaved Wind Flower*), large dark green palmate foliage, scarcely rising above the soil, with numerous golden yellow flowers nearly 2 inches across, on stems a foot in height. Strong established plants in pots, 6d. each; 5s. per doz.

Anemone palmata alba, a pure white variety of preceding, habit vigorous and remarkably free flowering, growing from 6 to 12 inches in height, flowers large, of a glistening white, on stems a foot in height; useful for cutting. Was awarded a First-class Certificate by the Royal Botanic Society. Strong plants in pots, 9d.; 7s. 6d. doz. *See* fig. above.

Anemone pulsatilla (*The Pasque Flower*). A charming species, admirably suited for the rockwork or the open border, especially in chalky soils; flowers deep rich purple, clothed on the exterior with long silky hairs, the carpels terminating in a long silky tuft. 9d. each; 8s. per doz. Seed 6d. pkt.

Anemone ranunculoides (*Yellow Wood Anemone*). Producing masses of golden yellow flowers early in spring. 9d each.

Anemone rivularis, very distinct and ornamental, flowers pure white, on branching heads, with purple anthers, growing about 2 feet in height in a damp position. 9d. each.; 8s. doz.

Anemone sylvestris, almost a fac-simile of *Anemone japonica alba,* flowering in early Summer instead of Autumn, flowers large, pure white and drooping, very free growing and a grand plant for naturalizing. 9d. each; 8s per doz. *See* fig. page 13.

Anemone vernalis, very distinct dwarf species; colour white, flushed purple; calyx thickly covered with brown silky hairs; most conspicuous and easily grown. 1s. 6d. *See* fig., p. 11.

Anthericum Liliago (*St Bernard's Lily*), a pretty perennial, bearing numerous branching spikes of starry white flowers. 6d. each; 5s. per doz. Seed, 3d. pkt.

Anemone Sylvestris See page 12.   *Aquilegia glandulosa.*

Anthericum graminifolium, a very graceful, free-growing, hardy perennial, flowers pure white, on long slender branching stems, very pretty for vases, etc. 9d. each; 8s. per doz.

Anthericum Liliastrum, spikes of pure white flowers, 2 feet in height, issuing from tufts of long narrow grass-like foliage, flowers 2 inches long, deliciously fragrant ; one of the most beautiful of our late spring-flowering perennials. 9d. each ; 8s. per doz.

Anthericum Liliastrum major, the large form of *St. Bruno's Lily*, flowers pure white, 2 inches in length, produced in great abundance; one of the best perennials in the whole of my collection, perfectly hardy and can be grown anywhere ; indispensable for cutting. 1s. each; 10s. 6d. per doz. Seed, 1s. per pkt. *See* fig. page 10.

Anthericum Algeriense, a large form of *A. Liliago*, large tufts of grassy foliage and numerous spikes of white flowers : very graceful, and a really first-class plant. 9d. each ; 8s. per doz.

Apios tuberosa, a rampant tuberous-rooted climbing plant ; curious purple flowers. 9d. each.

Aquatic and Bog Plants. *See* pages 60 to 63.

Aquilegia californica hybrida, very distinct, growing about 2½ft., bearing a profusion of bright scarlet and orange flowers. 9d. each ; 8s. doz. Seed, 6d. pkt.

Aquilegia chrysantha. Grows 2½ft. high, forming a bush from 2 to 3ft. across, covered for two months with numerous golden-yellow flowers with long spurs. 9d. ; 8s. doz. Seed, 6d. pkt.

Aquilegia cœrulea hybrida. This is a strain of unparalleled beauty, hybrids between *A. cærulea* and *A. chrysantha*, having similar shaped flowers but much larger. All are very distinct, varying from creamy-white to intense blue and rosy purple ; the combination of colours is grand, and there are scarcely two alike, and when seen in a mass is one of the most lovely sights imaginable. 9d. each ; 8s. doz. Seed, 1s. pkt.

Aquilegia glandulosa, one of the most beautiful and exquisite of all our hardy perennials. Flowers large, rich deep blue, with a pure white corolla, rendering it very conspicuous ; one of the most effective plants in my collection. 9d. each ; 8s. doz. Seed, 1s. pkt.

Aquilegia vulgaris alba, a pure white variety ; a good border plant. 6d. each ; 4s. per doz.

Arabis albida variegata, an edging or bedding plant, foliage prettily variegated. 6d. ea.; 5s. doz.

Arenaria purpurascens, a Pyrenean alpine plant, very dwarf; flowers purple. 9d. ; 7s. 6d. doz.

Armeria plantaginea rubra.   *Armeria Cephalotes rubra.*

Arnebia Echioides *(Prophet's Flower)*. Interesting & showy Borage-wort, about 18in. in height and as much through, producing flowers regularly three times between May and September. The flowers when first open are of a bright golden-yellow with five black blotches which gradually disappear on the second day, the flowers gradually changing to a pale yellow, so that on each plant will be found flowers of every shade of yellow, some with blotches and some without. It is perfectly hardy, easily grown, and a plant that should be found in every collection. Strong plants, 3s. 6d.; smaller, 1s. 6d. & 2s. 6d. each.

Arnica montana, a charming perennial "Composite," bearing large orange yellow flowers, on stems 9 inches in height. 9d. each.

Aronicum Scorpioides, this is a very showy perennial from the Pyrenees, producing large deep yellow Aster-like flowers, frequently 3 to 4 inches in diameter. The flowers are borne on very short stems. It is exceedingly showy, and quite hardy. 1s. each.

Armeria *(Giant Thrifts)*. Every one is more or less acquainted with the common *Sea Pink* or *Thrift*, a plant common in many districts, used generally as edging plants, or dotted about on the Rockery or border. The *Giant Thrifts* differ principally from these in their more robust growth, larger heads of flower and more brilliant colours. They form large tufts of long grassy foliage, varying considerably in length and width, from which isssue long, naked, wiry stems from 6 to 24 inches in height, terminating with large globular heads of various coloured flowers. They flower from May to August, producing flowers in endless quantities, and are invaluable for the Rockery and Border, and for cutting.

One of each of the following 4 varieties for 2s. 6d.

Armeria Cephalotes rubra, long narrow foliage, forming tufts a foot across, stems 18 inches in height, flower heads large, of a deep rich red. Strong plants, 9d. each; 8s. doz.

Armeria plantaginea rubra, similar in colour to above, stems taller and stouter, and the foliage very broad, similar to the "Plantain," from which it takes its specific name; this should be in every collection. Strong plants 9d.; 8s. doz.

Armeria plantaginea rosea, a fac-simile of preceding, with large rose-colored flowers. 9d.; 8s. dz.

Armeria bracteata rubra. This is a very marked plant, distinct in character from all, in fact, is one of the prettiest rock, border, or edging plants in my collection. It forms compact tufts of deep green, glossy foliage, and numerous stems 6 inches in height bearing bright crimson flowers, with numerous bracts, from 1 to 2 ins. in length, issuing from beneath the flowers. 9d. each; 8s. doz 50s. per 100.

Asclepias tuberosa.   *Aster alpinus speciosus.*

Arum Æthiopicum. *See* Calla.

Arundo. *See* Collections of Bamboos and Grasses, pages 58 and 59.

Asclepias incarnata, a good perennial for shrubbery borders, &c., flowers pink in large heads, sweetly scented. Bees are exceedingly fond of this plant. 9d. Seed, 6d. pkt.

Asclepias tuberosa, compact umbels of brilliant orange-coloured flowers on stems 2 feet high, each producing several heads of flower, and lasting a considerable time in bloom. One of the showiest of our autumnal flowers, and deserving of extensive cultivation. It is quite hardy, and grows freely in any soil, and is a plant I can highly recommend. 9d. Seed 6d. pkt.

Asphodelus luteus, an ornamental perennial, growing from 3 to 4ft. in height, producing spikes of bright yellow flowers, and in bloom for a considerable time. 9d. each. Seed, 3d. pkt.

Asphodelus luteus plenus, a double flowering variety of preceding; very rare. 2s. 6d.

Aster alpinus speciosus. This plant has far exceeded my expectations, and is admitted by everyone to be one of the finest for many years past, and one I cannot too strongly recommend. It forms dense prostrate tufts, from which issue stems 6 to 9 inches in height, forming a beautiful compact mass, literally covered with large circular flowers of a lovely rich violet, measuring 4 to 5 inches across, and continuing in full perfection all through the early summer months. It is perfectly hardy, easily grown, and should be found in every collection. Awarded First-class Certificate by the R.H.S. 1s.; 10s. doz. *See* fig. above.

Aster alpinus rubrus (*new*). Another very distinct variety, somewhat similar in habit to preceding, but with flowers of a delicate puce. It is a fine companion to preceding, and useful either as a border or rock plant; stock very limited. 2s. 6d. each.

Asters, a fine selection of Michaelmas Daisies will be found in this Catalogue. *See* Index.

Aubrietia Campbelli, improved, a vigorous growing variety of *A. Campbelli,* with large deep violet purple-coloured flowers; fine for spring bedding. 6d.; 5s. doz.

Aubrietia Leichtlini, by far the most beautiful of any of the spring bedding plants I have seen, and certainly the finest red hardy spring flower in cultivation. It is as hardy as the old "*purpurea,*" equally as free flowering, but of a bright crimson colour, changing to red, the only one of this colour in the genus, and is a great favourite with everyone. 9d. each; 8s. doz. Seed, 1s. pkt.

Baptisia Australis, a strong growing perennial, having spreading branching stems 3 to 4 feet in height, terminating with racemes of blue flowers. 9d. each. Seed, 6d. per pkt.

Bambusa. *See* pages 58 and 59.

Begonias. My catalogue of these was published in January, and may still be had on application; it is unquestionably the largest and best catalogue, and represents one of the finest collections in existence.

Bocconia cordata. one of the finest of our hardy foliage plants, admirably adapted for planting among shrubs, etc.; perfectly hardy, 6 to 8 feet high, flowers in terminal panicles, creamy white. 9d. each. Seed, 6d. pkt.

Bousingaultia basseloides, a pretty rapid climbing tuberous plant, flowers small in large clusters, pure white, and sweet scented. 9d.; 8s. per doz.

Bupthalmum salicifolium, a fine showy border or exhibition plant, forming neat symmetrical bushes 3 feet high, covered with large golden yellow blossoms. 6d. each. Seed, 3d. pkt.

Calandrinia umbellata, a charming evergreen shrub, scarcely exceeding 3 inches, producing flowers of an intense magenta-crimson colour. 6d.; 5s. doz. Seed, 6d. pkt.

Callirhoe involucrata, perhaps the prettiest trailing perennial in cultivation, bearing in prodigal profusion large beautiful violet-crimson flowers. 6d.; 5s. doz. Seed, 6d.

Callirhoe lineariloba, new and charmingly pretty trailing plant, forming a compact, prostrate mass of deeply divided foliage, literally covered with large deep purple and white Malva-like blossoms, from June to October; admirably adapted for the brows of rocks, or the front row in a sunny border. 9d.; 8/- doz. Seed 6d.

Calystegia pubescens plena.

Caltha palustris fl. pl. (*Double Marsh Marigold*), one of the most attractive of our early flowering bog plants; flowers very double and golden-yellow. 9d.; 8/- doz.

Caltha palustris plenus monstrosus, purplish green foliage and immense golden-yellow flowers, exceedingly double, distinct from the old variety and very rare. 2/6 each.

Calystegia pubescens plena, so many flowers are, by an unwarrantable abuse of the word, described "double," which have the merest claims to the designation, that a little scepticism as to its applicability to the plant under consideration may be pardoned. I can state, however, for the benefit of those unacquainted with this plant, that it is exceptionally double, remarkably free-flowering, producing an immense number of large double rose-coloured blossoms. It is a double variety of the large purple flowered Bind-weed, exceptionally free growing in almost any soil or situation, although a sunny one is preferable, and must be considered one of the prettiest climbers in cultivation. *See* fig. above. 9d.; 8s. doz.

Calystegia incarnata, delicate rose. 6d.; 5/- doz. | **Calystegia grandiflora,** snow-white. 6d.

Campanula abietina, one of the handsomest among the *Dwarf Hare Bells* in cultivation. The deep purple flowers flushed with crimson, form an hitherto unknown shade in this family, It is dwarf and densely compact, throwing up numerous slender wiry stems from 9 to 12in. in height, and produced in great profusion all through the summer months. It is exceedingly effective, and indispensable for the front of the border or in the rock garden. 9d.; 8/- doz.

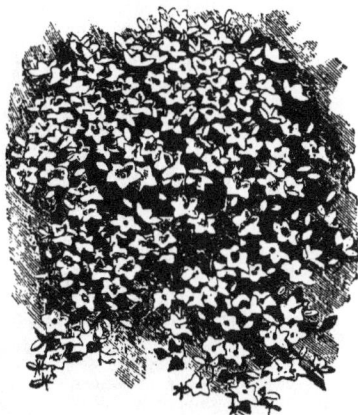

Campanula isophylla alba.   *Campanula dahurica (speciosa.)*

Campanula carpatica, one of the most distinct and beautiful among the Bell-flowers, the individual blooms are amongst the largest in the family. It is remarkable for its compact, densely set habit, and for yielding a fine display of lovely porcelain-blue blossoms. In its colour, habit, and season, it is without a rival; an effective dwarf border or rock-work plant, and easily grown anywhere. 6d. Seed, 3d. per pkt.

Campanula carpatica alba. This is a fac-simile of the preceding, only the flowers are pure white, contrasting exquisitely with the parent. 6d.; 5/- doz. Seed, 3d. pkt.

Campanula cordata (alliariæfolia), of the somewhat restricted number of white forms, this is one of the finest and certainly one of the most amenable to cultivation. The flowers are creamy white, borne on long graceful stems 2 ft. in height. 6d.; 5/- doz. *See* fig. page 18.

Campanula dahurica (speciosa), one of the showiest and most desirable, and undoubtedly one of the most remarkable and distinct of the Hare Bells. From a tenacious perennial root, it throws up many strong stems about 18 inches in height, terminating in aggregated clusters of rich purple flowers; one of the finest hardy plants in cultivation, invaluable for cutting purposes. *See* fig. above. 9d.; 8/- doz.

Campanula dahurica alba (speciosa), one of the finest novelties of the season, a fac-simile of preceding but with pure white flowers, a grand acquisition to our border perennials, stock very limited. 3/6 each.

Campanula fragilis, an invaluable free blooming procumbent species, flowers pale blue in loose corymbs, a gem for the rock garden, and very elegant as a basket plant. 9d.; 8/- doz. Seed, 1/-

Campanula garganica, a pretty rock or pot plant, forming sheets of blue flowers, with a starry white eye. 9d.

Campanula grandis, a fine old-fashioned perennial; habit bushy, 3 feet in height, composed of numerous spikes, thickly set with large blue Salver-shaped flowers. 6d.

Campanula isophylla alba. Although an old variety it is comparatively a scarce plant in our gardens. It is of a dwarf trailing habit, having large pure white flowers produced in endless profusion, and measuring 2 inches across. As a pot or basket plant it is admirably adapted, and can easily be grown in a cottage window, conservatory, border or rockery. It is a plant I have every confidence in strongly recommending. **Was awarded a F.C.C.** by the R.H.S. 9d.; 8/- doz. *See* fig. above.

B

Campanula Mariesi (Platycodon).   *Campanula cordata (alliariæfolia).* See page 17.

Campanula grandis alba. This is a beautiful snow-white form of *C. grandis;* a very vigorous grower, with a profuse flowering habit. Its pure clear white colour is an invaluable acquisition to the family, either for decoration or cutting purposes. 9d.; 8s. doz. Seed, 3d.

Campanula grandiflora (Platycodon) Wahlenbergia (*Chinese Bellflower*). Although the time has long gone by when this plant could be called a novelty, yet it is still very rare in gardens. It is the admiration of all who know it, and ought to be in every collection. Its stout, fleshy stems, glaucous foliage, and balloon-shaped flowers (before expansion), distinguish it at a glance from every other Hare Bell. Its most striking feature is the gigantic glaucous blue, balloon-like blossoms, the colour being equally apparent on both surfaces, which shows to great advantage on the intense blue ground. When fully expanded they are 4 or more inches across, and are borne in considerable numbers. a plant of average size producing 50 flowers. It is inferior to no other autumn flowering plant, and I have much pleasure in again offering it. Fine strong flowering plants, 9d.; 8s. doz. Seed, 3d.

Campanula grandiflora alba, similar in habit to preceding, but with pure white flowers; a fine companion plant. 1s. Seed, 3d.

Campanula grandiflora "Mariesi." This is a very typical Japanese plant, and one held in high esteem by the Japanese. It is distinct from any other plant in cultivation, only growing from 9 to 12 inches in height, composed of numerous rigid stems each terminating with large inflated blue flowers. As a pot plant it is unique, the flowers being so abundant as to almost cover the plant; on the rockery or front row of herbaceous border it is grand; one of the most distinct plants in the whole of my collection. 1/6 each. Seed 1/- pkt. *See* fig. above.

Campanula Hendersoni, a hybrid Bell-flower of great merit, possessing the advantage of flowering throughout the summer. The flowers are large and very numerous, of a pretty mauve colour, growing about 12 inches, forming a pretty pyramidal bush. It is very vigorous in growth, perfectly hardy, very distinct and can be strongly recommended. 9d. & 1s.

Campanula latifolia alba, one of the best of our border Campanulas. producing stout erect stems about 2½ft. high, bearing large pure white flowers in great abundance. 9d. Seed 3d. pkt.

Campanula macrantha, a vigorous growing border plant, forming an erect pyramidal bush 3 to 4ft. high, flowers purplish-blue, as large as the old *Canterbury Bell.* I have every confidence in recommending this either for the border or naturalizing, &c. 9d.; 8s. doz. *See* fig. p. 20.

Campanula muralis *(Portenschlagiana),* charming little hillocks of light green foliage smothered with pale blue flowers, a valuable pot, rock, or border plant. 9d.

Campanula nitida alba, dwarf evergreen species, large white flowers on spikes 9ins. high. 1s.

Campanula persicifolia coerulea plena (*The old double Blue Peach-leaved Bell-flower.*) A neat border plant, and one that should be found in every collection. 9d

Campanula persicifolia alba plena.
From "Garden Work."

Campanula persicifolia alba grandiflora.

Campanula persicifolia alba plena (*The double white Peach-leaved Bell-flower*). There are few plants that can vie with this lovely Campanula. It is one of the very best of this genus. The flowers are pure white in long close spikes 2 feet high, very double, resembling a column of double white Camellia-like flowers. It is exceedingly free flowering, and grand for cutting purposes, thriving well in almost any soil or situation, and a plant I can strongly recommend. The capital illustration given above will convey a slight idea of the beauty to those who do not know the plant. 6d.; 5s. doz. Strong clumps from ground, 9d.; 8s. doz. Seed, 1s.

Campanula persicifolia alba grandiflora. This is a very marked plant, and although it is simply a variety of the old white Peach-leaved Campanula, yet it is one that I cannot too strongly recommend. It differs from all others by the enormous number of flowers, immense size, and of the purest white imaginable. As a decorative plant there is nothing to beat it, erect sturdy habit, easily grown, and perfectly hardy; it was awarded First-Class Certificate. 1s.; 10s. 6d. doz. *See* fig. above.

Campanula persicifolia coronata alba, a very showy and attractive variety, with large white flowers, with a circular lobed frill, slightly recurved at the base of the flower. Commonly called the *Cup and Saucer Hare-Bell.* 9d.

Campanula pulla, one of the prettiest dwarf Hare Bells, forming, in cool spots, carpets of the loveliest verdure; numerous stems 2 to 3 inches in height, terminating with drooping deep purple flowers, very charming when seen in masses. 9d.; 7s. 6d. doz.

Campanula pumila alba, a neat and pretty rock plant, forming sheets of pure white drooping bell-shaped flowers. 6d.; 5s. doz.

Campanula pyramidalis (*Chimney Campanula*), a noble plant for the back of the herbaceous border, or for pot culture, forming a pyramid composed of numerous stems 4 to 5 feet in height, each stem being crowded with large blue Salver-like flowers. *See* fig. page 20. 6d. Seed, 3d. packet.

Campanula macrantha. See page 18.   *Campanula pyramidalis.* See page 19.

Campanula pyramidalis alba, similar to the preceding, but with white flowers. This is extensively grown in pots. 9d. Seed, 3d. packet.

Campanula Rhomboidea fl. pl., a very showy plant, producing slender stems 12 inches in height, supporting numerous deep blue flowers exceedingly double. 9d.

Campanula Scheuchzeri, a neat and attractive plant, producing stems from 12 to 15 inches in height, supporting numerous deep blue bells. The whole of the plant is very hirsute, giving it a peculiar greyish appearance, and is one of the most characteristic of this family. A fine plant for almost any situation on the rockwork or border. 1s. each.

Campanula Soldanellæflora, having slender stems about one foot in height, bearing numerous pale blue semi-double flowers, beautifully cut; a pretty plant for the rockwork or border. 9d.; 8s. doz.

Campanula turbinata is a dwarf compact growing species, having short erect stems, bearing large solitary Salver-shaped flowers of a rich bluish-purple colour. It grows with the greatest freedom in any light loamy soil, forming a charming rock or border plant. 1s. each.

Campanula urticifolia alba plena (*The Nettle-leaved Harebell*), a very decorative plant, compact and very floriferous. 9d. Seed, 6d. pkt.

Campanula Van Houttei, a charming hybrid; one of the finest and most showy of this extensive genus, erect stems 2 feet, bearing immense blue flowers 2 inches in length. 9d.

Campanula Van Houttei pallida (*Verschaffelti*), a counterpart of preceding, but with pale lavender-coloured flowers. 9d.

      6 distinct varieties, 3s. 6d.; 12 distinct varieties, 8s.

Cannas, a grand collection. *See* my *Florists' Flower Catalogue.*

Carnations and Cloves, *see* my *Florists' Flower Catalogue.*

Carnivorous Plants, *see* page 82.

Catananche cœrulea, a good perennial; hardy, easily grown, wonderfully free blooming and valuable for cutting. 6d.; 5s. doz. Seed, 3d. pkt.

Catananche cœrulea bicolor, similar to preceding in growth, &c., but with white flowers marked purple in the centre. 6d.; 5s. doz. Seed, 3d. pkt.

Centaurea dealbata, large rose-coloured flowers, useful for wild garden, &c. 9d. Seed, 6d. pkt.

Centaurea glastifolia, somewhat resembling *C. macrocephala*, but more graceful in habit. 1s.

Chrysanthemum maximum (true). *See* page 22.

Centaurea macrocephala, a stately and ornamental plant, effective either in foliage or flower. The leaves are large and massive, produced from the base to the point from which the flowers issue; these are very large and of a rich golden-yellow colour. It is very useful for cutting, for the back row of the herbaceous border, among shrubs, or naturalizing in the wild garden. Figured in the *Gardeners' Chronicle*, Aug., 1886. 1s.; 10s. doz. Seed, 6d. pkt.

Centaurea montana (*Perennial Cornflower*), a very useful and effective group of plants, from 1 to 2 feet high; flowers red, white, blue, and purple, produced in great abundance during summer; invaluable for cutting and market purposes. Seed, 6d.

montana, blue, 6d. | montana alba, white, 6d. | montana rubra, red, 6d. | montana purpurea, 6d.

Cheiranthus Cheiri (*Single Wallflower*).—These can be supplied from early autumn until April:— Deep Crimson, fine strain. 2s. 6d. doz; 16s. 100. | New Dwarf Yellow. 2s. 6d. doz.; 16s. 100.

Cheiranthus Cheiri luteus & purpureus plenus. Many will hardly recognise the old-fashioned double Wallflowers under such a name. They are among the very oldest varieties, and in many parts of the country scarce a garden will be found without its double Wall-flowers. Against a wall they are very pretty, remarkably free blooming, and may be grown for years without any care or attention. Double Yellow, 6d.; 5s. doz. D'ble. Crim., 6d.; 5s. dz.

Cheiranthus alpinus, one of the finest of our spring flowers, either for massing, borders, or rock-work, forming dense cushions covered with numerous fragrant sulphur-coloured flowers. 6d; 5s.

Cheiranthus Marshalli, one of the finest of our spring flowers, either for massing, borders, or rockwork, forming dense masses covered with numerous fragrant orange-coloured flowers. 9d.; 8s. doz.

Chelone obliqua, a stately and handsome perennial, bearing numerous spikes, terminating in large aggregate flower-heads, of a rich violet-purple, in late summer and autumn. 9d.; 8s. doz. Seed, 3d. pkt.

Chelone glabra, a very distinct and interesting plant, flowers large in clustered heads of a creamy-white, in shape somewhat resembling an Antirrhinum; hardy, and easily grown, and will be an ornament to any border. 6d.; 5s. doz.

Chrysanthemum latifolium. This is one of the best of the large Marguerites; flowers 2 to 3 inches across, pure white with a yellow centre, invaluable for autumn decoration or for cutting purposes. It grows 3ft., forming a large bush covered with flowers for two months. 9d.; 8s. doz.

Chrysanthemum, summer-flowering varieties, *see* Catalogue published in January.

Chrysanthemum Leucanthemum semi-duplex, a peculiar double form of the Common May-weed, reminding one of some of the Japanese Chrysanthemums; flowers pure white, remarkably free flowering, grow in any position or soil; highly recommended as a first-class decorative or cutting variety.   Awarded a First-Class Certificate by the R.H.S.   9d.; 8/- doz.

Chrysanthemum maximum *(true)*. I have much pleasure in again offering this plant, which has proved to be a grand acquisition, and has met with universal approbation from every one who has had it. It is totally distinct from any other plant in cultivation, and is first-class for the decoration of the border or for cutting purposes. It is free growing, not more than 2 feet high, forming a large bush, which is literally smothered with pure white flowers of great substance and very symmetrical, and quite as large as *C. latifolium*. For cutting purposes it is held in the highest esteem, as the flowers last over a week when cut. I have every confidence in recommending it, and feel sure when better known it will be in great demand. *See* fig., page 21.   9d.; 8s. doz.

Chrysanthemum speciosum *(Leucanthemum)*, large pure white flowers on stems 1ft in height. A showy border plant, and very useful for cutting.   Strong plants, 6d.; 5s. doz.

Chrysanthemum uliginosum *(Pyrethrum)*, a strong growing showy, hardy perennial, pro-ducing in large quantities pure white Aster-like flowers about 3 inches in diameter; an invaluable plant for late summer and autumn decoration.   9d.; 7s. 6d. doz.   Seed, 6d. pkt.

Chrysobactron Hookeri, an interesting and showy Liliaceous plant, with long linear leaves of a dark green colour, and stout flower spikes thickly set with numerous bright yellow flowers; a fine plant for a shady border in peaty soil.   1s.

Cimicifuga racemosa, a very bold showy plant, and one rarely met with in cultivation. It is exceedingly handsome both in foliage and flower, having large biternate leaves deeply cut into segments & long drooping racemes of feathery white flowers.   Strong plants, 1s.; 10s. dz.

Clematis, in variety, *see* my Catalogue of Hardy Climbers.

Clematis coccinea, is of a neat slender growth, attaining to the height of 5 to 6ft in one season, flowering freely in the axils of the leaves, and at the extremity of the branches. The sepals are 4 in number, very thick and fleshy, about 1½ inches in length, bell-shaped at the base, but having the segments reflexed at the tip. The interior is a bright orange, while the exterior is an intense vermilion, and the plant when covered with flowers has a most gorgeous appearance.   1s. 6d. each.

Cistus, a very effective and useful group of Hardy Shrubs, principally from the sunny shores of the Mediterranean, and yet quite hardy in this country. They are easily grown, perfectly hardy, producing an abundance of most brilliant-coloured flowers, and continuing in bloom for a long period. The following are the best and can all be thoroughly recommended.

Cistus florentinus, this is a gem and should be grown in window boxes, in pots, in the borders, on the rockery, in pans, in fact there is scarcely a place for which it is not suited. It is a dwarf evergreen shrub scarcely exceeding a foot in height, which is completely covered with large snow white flowers.   1s. each; 10s. 6d. doz.

    Crispus, 1s. | **Clusii**, 1s. 6d. | **formosus**, 1s. | **Ladaniferus**, 1s. | **Laurifolius**, 1s.
       Lusitanicus, 1s. | **Salvæfolius**, 6d. | **Undulatus**, 9d.

6 distinct varieties of above for 4s. 6d.

Clintonia Andrewsiana, one of the most beautiful of the Californian Lilyworts, having large ovate glossy-green leaves and terminal umbels of deep rose-coloured flowers, followed by pretty deep blue berries. It has a decided character of its own, and for a moist shady nook a most interesting plant.   2s. 6d. and 3s. 6d. each.

Codonopsis ovata, an Himalayan species with large bell-shaped flowers of a beautiful metallic blue; the interior beautifully veined and blotched with white and yellow. Grows best in a light sandy soil.   9d.

Convolvulus mauritanicus, a free growing trailing plant, covering the ground with its abundant foliage and numerous blue flowers as large as a florin; a useful basket or rock plant.   1s.   Seed, 6d. pkt.

Coreopsis grandiflora *(true)*. I am pleased at being able to offer this long lost species, and to be the means of re-introducing a most beautiful hardy perennial. It is totally distinct from *C. lanceolata*, and a far superior plant; and I am certain it will find its way into every collection, and will be acknowledged as one of the best perennials we have. It grows about 3 feet in height, having deeply pinnatifid leaves, the radical ones 12 to 18ins. in length. The stems are erect and rigid, producing flowers 2½ to 3ins. across, of a bright golden-yellow, flowering profusely from the end of June until late in September. It is a perennial, hardy, and for decoration or cutting, one of the best in my collection. *See* fig. on cover.   1s. 6d. each.   Seed, 1s. per packet.

Convallaria prolificans.   *Delphinium cashmerianum.*

Coreopsis lanceolata *(true)*, one of the most showy hardy perennials in cultivation; flowers large, bright golden-yellow, and produced in the greatest profusion. It will grow in any soil, and is invaluable for cutting purposes. 6d.; 5s. doz. Seed, 6d. per pkt.

Coreopsis verticillata, a slender growing species about 2ft. high, having the leaves in whorls, and divided into very narrow segments. The flowers are of a rich golden-yellow, 1in. across, exceedingly numerous ; one of the most distinct plants in my collection. 1s.

Cortusa Mathioli, closely allied to the Primulas ; pretty for a shady bed. 9d.; 8s. doz.

Convallaria prolificans, a new and very distinct variety of the *Lily of the Valley*, having large white flowers flushed with pink in the interior, on erect branching panicles, 2ft. long, rising from the large glabrous, oblong leathery leaves, and exhaling a much richer spicy fragrance than the common *Lily of the Valley*. It is quite hardy and a vigorous grower, and when established is a very effective plant. Strong plants, 1s. ; 10s. 6d. doz. *See* fig. above.

✗**Corydalis nobilis**, this noble species is distinguished by its remarkably large flowers, and is unquestionably the handsomest of the genus. The flowers are deep rich yellow, faintly flushed on the tips with green, with a very long spur. It blooms in early spring, and is a grand plant for a shady moist spot. 9d. & 1s. each.

Corydalis Scouleri, closely related to *C. nobilis*, but the leaves are more glaucous and more deeply divided with a greater number of divisions. Racemes large, bearing pretty rose-coloured flowers. 1s. 6d. each. **Cyclamen,** *see* page 69 of this Catalogue.

Cypripedium and other **Terrestrial Orchids,** *see* pages 72 to 75 of this Catalogue.

Dahlias, complete descriptive list published first week in April, free on application. Seed, 6d.

Daisies *(Bellis perennis)*, for full collection of these, *see* my Florists' Flower Catalogue.

Delphinium cardinale, the re-appearance of this good old plant will be acknowledged by all lovers of hardy plants as a great acquisition. It is totally distinct from *D. nudicaule*, being of a more vigorous habit, attaining 4 feet in height, the flowers larger, of a brighter scarlet, with a decided yellow centre. In habit it approaches the variety of *D. nudicaule elatior*, but the flowers are distinct from any form yet introduced. 1s. 6d. Seed, 1s. per pkt.

✗**Delphinium Cashmerianum**, this forms a tuft of dark green palmate foliage, not unlike *Anemone japonica*, having flowers from 1½ to 2ins. across, of a pale blue, 18 ins. in height. *See* fig. above. Strong, 6d. ; 5s. per doz. Seed, 6d. pkt.

Delphinium chinensis, a very pretty and effective group of plants about 1ft. in height, having branching stems, terminating with conspicuous blue flowers. 6d. ; 5s. doz.

Delphinium chinensis album, equally as effective as preceding, flowers pure white. 6d.; 5s. dz.

Dictamnus fraxinella.   *Doronicum plantagineum excelsum.*   See page 25.

Delphinium hybridum, a grand collection. For particulars, *see* my new Florists' Flower Catalogue, published with this edition. Seed, 6d. per pkt.

Delphinium nudicaule, a dwarf hardy perennial 18ins. in height, bearing numerous bright red flowers. When massed together they have a very telling effect. 9d.; 7s. 6d. doz. Seed, 6d.

Delphinium sulphureum (Zalil), an interesting and remarkably handsome species, the most remarkable acquisition to our list of Perennials for many years past. It has a beautiful branching habit, often reaching the height of 3 to 4 feet, forming a pyramidal bush composed of stiff, wiry stems, which are covered with flowers about an inch in diameter, of the most beautiful pure sulphur-yellow colour, from 40 to 50 blossoms being borne on each branch, presenting a magnificent aspect, and as proved perfectly hardy. The flowers are produced on the main stem in June, and are succeeded by the lateral branches later, so that the flowering time lasts from June to August. Strong plants, 3s. 6d. each. Seed, 1s. pkt.

Dianthus alpinus, tufts of dark green foliage, scarcely an inch in height, which are covered with deep rosy-crimson flowers as large as a florin. 1s. each. Seed, 1s. per pkt.

Dianthus barbatus magnificus *(Ware's Double Sweet William).* The *Chronicle,* speaking of this plant, says—"It is a remarkable plant not only for its deep crimson double flowers, but also for its dwarf habit, free flowering properties, and readiness of propagation." 9d.; 8s. doz.

Dianthus cæsius, a charming plant for the rockery or front row of the border, forming compact cushions of glaucous green foliage and rosy-pink flowers. 6d.; 5s. doz.

Dianthus cruentus, producing slender stems, one foot in height, supporting numerous blood-crimson flowers in clusters. 9d.

Dianthus glaciatis, a lovely alpine species, of a close dwarf habit, scarce an inch in height, covered with brilliant rosy-crimson flowers, unquestionably one of the most beautiful of the high Alpine Flora, and one easily grown. 1s. 6d.

Dianthus deltoides, 6d.   **Dianthus deltoides alba,** 6d.

NOTE.—*In addition to the above, I have many others equally useful; they are very pretty for the rockwork, or the front row of the herbaceous border, and thrive well in ordinary soil.* 6d.

Dictamnus fraxinella (*Burning Bush*). This remarkable plant is one of the most singularly interesting and beautiful herbaceous perennials in existence. It forms a neat erect stiff bush about 2½ft. in height, carrying long terminal racemes of curious red flowers, the whole plant emitting a strong balsamic scent, which readily ignites at certain periods, hence the name, "Burning Bush." 9d. & 1s.; 8s. & 10s. doz. Seed, 3d. (*See* fig. above).

Dictamnus fraxinella alba, similar to the preceding, but with white flowers, a first-class decorative plant, and very easily grown. 1s.; 10s. doz. Seed, 3d. packet.

Dielytra formosa, a charming spring-flowering plant, having delicate Fern-like foliage and red flowers. The foliage is very useful for cutting in early spring.

Dielytra spectabilis (*Bleeding Heart*), one of our best border plants, and unequalled for a cold house, flowers white and red. Strong flowering plants, 9d.; 8s. doz.

Dielytra spectabilis alba, this lovely plant is similar in every respect to the type, but with white flowers faintly flushed with pink. 2s. 6d.

Digitalis grandiflora, a yellow perennial Foxglove, quite hardy, easily grown, and forms an effective plant for any ordinary border. 9d. Seed, 3d. packet.

Doronicum Austriacum, a very effective spring-flowering perennial, growing 18 inches in height ; flowers large, of a bright golden yellow; grows in any ordinary soil and increases rapidly. 9d.; 8s. dz.

Doronicum Clusii. No plant can surpass, and very few can equal, the intense richness of this plant, when its countless numbers of rich yellow flowers are expanded. It rejoices in any kind of garden loam, where it will increase rapidly; is well worthy of the most extensive cultivation, being, perhaps, the most effective yellow Spring border plant known. 9d.; 7s. 6d. doz. Stronger plants 1s.; 10s. 6d. doz.

Doronicum plantagineum excelsum, a beautiful spring-flowering hardy perennial, having large golden-yellow flowers 4 inches in diameter, blooming in March and continuing at intervals during the whole of the season. It can also be had in bloom in January by lifting strong clumps and placing them in a cold house or frame. It is fond of plenty of moisture,

Echinacea purpurea.

and prefers a stiff soil; was figured and described in the *Garden*, and was awarded a First-class Certificate by the R.H.S. Strong plants, 9d. each; 7s. 6d. dz. *See* fig. page 24.

Draba, a small group of spring-flowering plants, forming compact cushions which are covered with white and yellow flowers; for the rockery they are unequalled.

     D. azoides, 9d. | D. gigas, 9d. | D. cuspidata, 1s.

Dracocephalum Ruprechti, grows about 1 foot in height, with whorls of light blue flowers in great profusion. 9d.; 8s. doz. Seed 6d. per packet.

Dracocephalum virginicum, a pretty erect-growing perennial, forming a number of stout stems about 2½ feet in height, and crowded for about two-thirds of the height with numerous bright pink flowers. It is quite hardy, and easily grown. 9d.

Dracocephalum virginicum album, a fac-simile of preceding, with white flowers. Has been awarded a First-class Certificate by the R.H.S. 9d.; 7s. 6d. doz.

Echinacea purpurea. A very uncommon and beautiful plant, and unquestionably one of the best of our autumn-flowering perennials, growing about 3 feet in height, with numerous deep reddish-purple flowers, with black centres, 3 to 4 inches across; a first-class border plant, and one I can recommend. (*See* fig. above). 1s. 6d. each.

Echinops ritro, a strong growing perennial from 3 to 4 feet in height, bearing an abundance of large solid globular heads of blue flowers, very ornamental. Strong plants, 9d. Seed, 6d. pkt.

Epigæa repens *(Mayflower* or *Ground Laurel).* This remarkable species and sole representative of the genus is distinguished by having flowers which, for delicacy of tint and spicy fragrance, are unequalled by any temperate plant in existence. It is of a dwarf creeping habit, and evergreen, forming, when well grown, patches 2 feet or more across. The flowers often terminate the branches, and are thickly set in axillary clusters all along the stems, from one to six in number, and are often an inch across, with neatly rounded petals, the colour being white or pale rose, varying in intensity in different specimens, from white to clear rose, but invariably of the most delicious fragrance. It is thoroughly hardy, requiring a moist position with a liberal supply of peat and sand. Established plants, 2s. 6d. & 3s. 6d. ea.

Epilobium angustifolium album. Very showy spikes of pure white flowers. 6d.

Epimedium *(Barren-wort).* Lovely genus of dwarf plants, forming neat clumps about 1 ft. high, of leathery leaves and graceful panicles of lovely flowers, white yellow, lilac, crimson, purple, and lavender. They grow best in light peaty soil, in partially shaded situations. 4 vars., 3s.

Eremurus himalaicus. Colossal in proportions and noble in bearing, a plant to be seen once and remembered for ever; one of the best of this little known genus. The illustration given of *E. robustus* will also apply to this, the great difference being in the colour of the flower. The massive stems attain to the height of 6 to 8 feet, two-thirds of which are covered with large white or creamy-white flowers, most evenly arranged so that there is no crowding. It requires a nice well-drained border, protected somewhat by shrubs, to prevent cold winds or late frosts injuring the young foliage. A few extra strong plants at 10s. 6d. each.

Eremurus robustus.

Eremurus Olgae, quite distinct in habit from any other species, and flowering from July till September, the last in bloom of this genus. The leaves are linear, stout, and almost erect, frequently covered with long filaments. The flower stem grows from 4 to 6 feet in height, covered with beautiful bright rose flowers and sweetly scented. Extra large plants, most of which will flower the first year, 15s. each.

Eremurus robustus. Visitors to my Nursery during the last few years will remember the magnificent specimens they have seen in bloom of this beautiful plant, spikes 9 to 10 ft. in height, with at least 4 ft. covered with bloom. Without a doubt this family is one of the greatest acquisitions for many years, and will in a short time become a great favourite. The figure given on page 26 will give a faint idea of the general character of the plant. The flowers are of a bright Peach colour, and very sweetly scented, remaining in bloom for 5 or 6 weeks. 3s. 6d., 5s., 7s. 6d., and 10s. each.

Eremurus turkestanicus. If not quite so beautiful as preceding, is nevertheless well worth growing ; the leaves are glaucous green, about 18 inches in length, producing slender spikes from 3 to 4 feet in height, with silky-white flowers. This is the earliest of all, flowering about the end of May. Strong plants, in pots, most of which will flower the first year. 2s. 6d. and 3s. 6d. each.

NOTE.—All the Eremuri are tuberous rooted plants like an Asphodel, and require a good well drained border, not too stiff, and planted so that the young foliage will be protected from cutting winds or early Spring frosts, and I would also suggest protecting roots during very severe weather.

Erigeron aurantiacum, comparatively new, and by far the best of the genus. It forms a tuft somewhat like *Aster alpinus*, stems 9 inches, bearing bright orange flowers as large as a crown piece. It flowers very freely, and will thrive in almost any soil, and can be strongly recommended. 9d. ; 8s. doz. Seed, 6d. pkt.

Erigeron grandiflorum, a dwarf spring-flowering plant, forming neat compact tufts, surmounted by numerous blue flowers 2 inches or more across. 6d.; 5s. doz.

Erigeron grandiflorum album, a showy dwarf, rock, or border plant, forming a cæspitose tuft of leaves and numerous white Aster-like flowers 2 inches across. This is often called *Aster alpinus albus*. 9d. ; 8s. doz.

Erigeron salsuginosus, a fine border perennial growing about 2 feet in height, literally smothered with large lilac-white blossoms, fine for cutting. 6d. each.

Erigeron speciosum superbum, a neat border perennial, about 3 feet, covered for a long time with large purple flowers, with a yellow centre; a fine plant for the autumn. 6d. ; 5s. doz.

Erodium Manescavi, a very handsome species, forming tufts of graceful foliage, from which issue numerous stems bearing umbels of purplish-red flowers an inch across. It is adapted for any situation on the rockwork or borders; flowering until autumn. 9d. ; 8s. doz.

Erpetion reniforme (*The Australian Violet*), a neat trailing plant, flowers blue and white ; very useful for a cool fernery. 9d. each.

Eryngium Oliverianum (amethystinum), a noble and handsome plant, sufficiently attractive for almost any situation in the flower border. It is as hardy as it is beautiful, and one that can be recommended as a first-class, strong growing border perennial. It grows about 3 feet, with handsome spiny, laciniated foliage, and heads of a lovely Amethystine-blue, the bracts, as well as the upper portion of the stem, being of the same pleasing colour. *See fig. page 28*. 1s. each.

Eryngium Alpinum, "*true,*" the finest of this family, and one of the most beautiful hardy plants in existence. A few only to offer at 3s. 6d. each.

Eryngium giganteum (*Ivory Thistle*), a noble and handsome plant, forming a large bush 2½ feet high, very rigid and symmetrical. The stems are glistening white, and the leaves and bracts all partake, more or less, of the same colour ; a remarkable plant and in great demand for decoration, the flowers lasting for years in a cut state. 1s. Seed, 6d. per packet.

Eryngium bromeliæfolium, foliage about 2 feet in length, very persistent, and spiny, throwing up rigid stems about 4 feet, of white flowers; a conspicuous plant for isolated positions on the lawn, or in a young state for dinner-table decorations. 9d. each; 8s. doz.

Eryngium pandanifolium, another noble species, having leaves 3 ft. in length, exceedingly spiny at the base, the spines measuring at least half-an-inch in length. The flower stem frequently attains 10 feet, bearing branching heads of reddish-violet flowers. 9d. ; 8s. doz.

Eupatorium purpureum, a gigantic perennial, when established attaining 8 to 10ft. in height, with branching heads of purple flowers 18 ins. across; very late in autumn. 9d. Seed, 6d.

Funkias, a beautiful genus of handsome foliage plants, comprising some of the most ornamental in cultivation. Their noble aspect, elegant outline, and bold Palm-like leaves, render them exceedingly attractive either for pot culture or for planting in the open ; they also form grand subjects for exhibition purposes. 6d. to 1s. 6d. each.

Six distinct Funkias to name for 4/-

Fuchsias, hardy, the entire collection will be found in my *Dahlia Catalogue*, published in April.

Gaillardias, a fine collection, *see* my Florist Flower Catalogue.

Gaultheria procumbens (*Creeping Winter Green*), a very pretty shrubby, creeping evergreen, with ovate leaves of a pleasing bronze colour, with nodding white axillary flowers, succeeded by bright red berries and very aromatic foliage. Nice plants, 1s. 6d.

Genista Andreana. I have much pleasure in calling attention to this sterling novelty. It is one of the most remarkable shrubs that has been introduced for many years, being a wild variety of the common Broom, *Genista Scoparia,* and was found growing wild in the north of France. It is equally as free flowering as the common yellow variety, the upper petals being of a rich golden yellow, while the lower ones are of a rich velvety crimson, a remarkable combination and exceedingly effective. This will become one of the most popular hardy flowering shrubs in cultivation, is a favourite with everyone, and has been awarded highest honours wherever exhibited. 2s. 6d. each. Ex. strong, 3s. 6d. each.

Gentiana acaulis (*Gentianella*), charming cushions of glossy foliage, from which issue numerous erect bell-shaped flowers of an intense blue. *See* fig. page 29. 6d. each; 5s. doz. Large clumps, 1s.; 10s. doz.

Gentiana acualis var. excisa, similar to preceding in habit, but much freer flowering and lighter in shade. 1s.

Gentiana alpina, a pretty high alpine species, flowers sky-blue, varying in shade. 2s. 6d. each.

Gentiana Andrewsi (*The Closed Gentian*), this grows about 2ft., producing numerous flowers in terminal and axillary clusters; the flowers never expand, remaining as it were in bud, and are about 1½ inches in length, of a rich purplish-blue, striped with white. 1s. Seed, 6d.

Eryngium Oliverianum (amethystinum), see page 27.

Gentiana Auverensis, one of the most distinct of this interesting family and is easily grown. In general appearance it resembles a gigantic form of *G. pneumonanthe,* producing slender erect stems terminating with clusters of pale blue, well expanded flowers. 1s. 6d.

Gentiana asclepiadea, a showy border plant, having slender stems 2ft. in height producing abundance of purplish-blue flowers in long terminal clusters, quite hardy, and thriving well in the ordinary border. 1s. each.

Gentiana bavarica, one of the most lovely of the Gentians; tufts of small Box-like foliage and brilliant blue flowers; more beautiful than the *Gentiana verna.* I am very pleased at being able to offer fine strong blooming plants of this rare species. 2s. 6d.

Gentiana calycosa, a pretty American species, growing about 1 foot, each stem supporting 3 to 4 lovely sky-blue flowers one inch in length. 1s. 6d.

Gentiana cruciata, a vigorous species, growing 9 inches, flowers deep blue, in whorls. 6d.; 5s. doz.

Gentiana septemfida.   *Gentiana acaulis.* See page 28.

Gentiana decumbens (*new*), another species from Turkestan, belonging to the *Pneumonanthe* group; flowers sky-blue in clustered heads; a well marked species. 1s. 6d.

Gentiana lutea (*The Giant Yellow Gentian*), whorls of numerous bright yellow flowers on stems 3 to 5 feet in height; distinct from all others of this family. 1s.

Gentiana Pneumonanthe (*The Heath Gentian*), numerous slender stems 6 to 9 inches high, with abundance of light blue flowers 1½ inches in length, interior dark blue. 9d.

Gentiana septemfida, a very handsome dwarf species, growing about 12 inches, bearing umbels of bright blue flowers, growing freely on the rockwork or border in a half-shady situation in good rich sandy loam. *See* fig. above. 1s.

Gentiana verna, an indigenous species, surpassed by none of the higher *European alpines*, forming dense dwarf tufts of intense brilliant blue flowers with a white eye. It grows freely in deep rich fibry loam, and is very partial to limestone. Established plants in pots, 1s. each; 9s. doz.

Geranium argenteum, rosettes of silvery-grey foliage, with large rose-coloured flowers, slightly veined, growing on stems 2 inches in height; a first-class rock plant, and very rare. 1s. 6d. each.

Geranium armenium, a neat symmetrical plant about 2ft. in height, bearing large deep purplish crimson flowers. It is adapted either for the rockery or border, and is a first-class plant. 1s.

Geranium cinerium, a showy rock or border plant, forming tufts of silvery foliage, adorned with numerous white flowers veined with purple. 1s.

Geranium Endresse, this is one of the brightest and most effective of this family, the flowers are exceedingly numerous, of a bright rose colour; a really first-class perennial, deserving of more extended cultivation. Clumps, 9d.; 8s. doz. Seed, 1s.

Geranium ibericum, the best of the strong-growing varieties, forming pretty symmetrical bushes 2ft. in height, flowers as large as a florin, of a rich purplish-blue; a fine companion to preceding. Strong plants from ground, 9d.

Geranium pratense album plenum, a shrubbery plant, bold foliage, and double white flowers, an attractive variety. 9d.

Geranium sanguineum, a highly ornamental border or rock plant; the flowers are large, of a deep crimson-purple, and are produced in great profusion the whole of the summer. 9d.

Geranium sanguineum var. lancastriense, a very distinct variety resembling above, but with beautiful flesh coloured flowers veined with purple. A first-class rock plant. 9d. Seed, 1s.

Geum coccineum plenum, this grand old plant is too well known to thousands to require either description or eulogium, and those of my patrons who are in need of a really first-rate decorative or cutting plant, I strongly urge them to plant this old-fashioned "*Scarlet Geum*" in quantity. The flower heads are large, produced in countless numbers, and of the most intense dazzling scarlet, and semi-double, invaluable for cutting or border decoration, and no collection is complete without it. 9d.; 8s. doz. Seed, 3d. per pkt.

Geum miniatum, this is a very distinct variety, bearing some resemblance to the well-known *Geum coccineum*, similar in habit, but the foliage larger and the flower stems taller and more branched, having large single flowers of a bright orange-scarlet, and remarkably showy; a really first-class plant, and distinct from any other hardy plant in my collection. 9d.

Geum montanum, a charming rock or border plant, forming compact tufts and producing abundance of showy golden-yellow flowers on stems 12 inches in height; a first-class perennial, and easily grown. 1s.; 10s. 6d. doz.

Gillenia trifoliata, forms an erect bush 3ft. high, having slender panicles of white flowers. 1s. and 1s. 6d.

Globularia cordifolia, globular heads of pretty blue flowers, quite hardy, easily grown, and well adapted for the rockery. 9d.

Globularia trichosantha, globular heads of dark blue flowers, issuing from the tufts of dark green leathery foliage; very pretty, and easily grown. 6d.

Gloxinias and **Gladiolus**, *see* my Begonia Catalogue, which can be had on application.

Gnaphalium Leontopodium ("*The Edelweiss*"). This is as easily grown as any ordinary perennial either from plants or seed, but should be planted on the rockery in very sandy soil mixed with stones. It is a quaint plant both in foliage and flower, and well worthy of cultivation. 9d.; 8s. doz. Seed, 6d. per pkt.

Geum coccineum plenum.

Gunnera manicata, a gigantic plant, and one of the most striking that possibly can be imagined. It should be found in every garden where sufficient space can be made for its reception. The leaves are from 12 to 20 feet in circumference, borne upon stout footstalks from 4 to 6 feet in height. It is perfectly hardy, and prefers a damp, shady situation. 3s. 6d.

Gunnera scabra, a gigantic species, producing leaves from 4 to 5ft. in diameter, on stout petioles 3 to 6ft. in height. It is quite hardy, and forms a noble plant in conspicuous positions on the lawn, in moist shady situations, besides running streams, &c. Strong plants, 2s. 6d.

Gynerium, *see* List of Grasses, pages 58 and 59.

Gypsophila prostrata, a charming rock plant, about 6 inches, with small white flowers. 6d.

Gypsophila paniculata, a most beautiful old-fashioned perennial, possessing a grace not found in any other perennial, and attracting the eye of every one. When in bloom it forms a symmetrical mass 2 to 3 feet in height, and as much through, of minute pure white flowers, forming a beautiful gauze-like appearance. For cutting purposes it is exquisite, especially in combination with high-coloured flowers, and some most lovely effects have been produced at the various exhibitions. I consider that it is indispensable in every garden, and where space admits should be grown in quantity for cutting. It is hardy, lasts for years and thrives in any soil or situation. *See* fig., page 31. 6d.; 5s. doz. Seed, 3d. per packet.

Helleborus, a collection of both Christmas and Lenten Roses will be found on pages 70 to 71.

Helianthus, or **Perennial Sunflowers**. *See* pages 76 to 78.

Gypsophilla paniculata. See page 30.   *Helenium Bolanderi.*

Habenaria, *see* List of Orchids. | **Harpalium rigidum,** *see* "Helianthus."

Haberlea rhodopensis, this elegant little alpine plant is rarely met with even in the choicest collections of hardy perennials. It is a beautiful companion to *Ramondia pyrenaica,* but altogether a much superior plant, growing in dense rosettes of wrinkled leaves, producing freely, numerous Gloxinia-like flowers on dark brown stems; the interior is pale lilac with a yellow speckled throat. The same treatment as *Ramondia pyrenaica.* 3s. 6d. ;

Helianthella quinquenervis (Helianthus occidentalis) (*Gray*). This is a remarkably pretty plant, not only on account of its neatness of habit, but also for its free flowering properties. It is closely allied to the Helianthus, forming neat symmetrical bushes 2½ feet in height, composed of slender stems, bearing a profusion of large, rich, golden-yellow flowers with a dark centre, and invaluable for cutting early in summer. It is quite hardy, and a plant I can strongly recommend as a first-class Perennial. 2s. each.

Helianthemum, (*Rock Rose*), a genus of ornamental evergreen flowering shrubs, forming compact bushes from 3 to 9 inches in height, covered with large flowers of every shade of colour, both single and double; invaluable for hot dry situations on the rockwork or border.
6 in 6 vars., 3s. 6d. | 12 in 6 vars., 5s. | 12 in 12 vars., 6s. | 50 in 12 vars., 21s.

Helenium autumnale, a strong growing autumn-flowering perennial, having large yellow flowers, 3 inches across, very useful for cutting for church decoration. 9d.; 8s. doz.

Helenium Bolanderi, a really first-class autumn-blooming perennial, similar to *H. pumilum,* but having larger flowers, deeper in colour, with a black disc, and taller in growth; a rare and very beautiful plant, and one I can very strongly recommend, not only on account of its beauty, but for its freedom of growth, hardiness and easy cultivation. 1s. 6d.

Helenium pumilum, a well-known autumn-flowering variety, growing about 18 inches and smothered with golden-yellow flowers 2ins. across, nearly the whole of summer and autumn; a grand plant for cutting or for Exhibition, is grown by acres for Covent Garden. Strong, 9d.

Helenium grandicephalum striatum, a long lost plant which I have pleasure in re-introducing, although a much smaller stock than I usually offer, hence the necessity of securing early. Height 4 feet, very robust erect habit, flowers on large branching heads, deep orange, irregularly striped and blotched with crimson. 1s. 6d. each; 15s. doz.

Hepatica. This collection will be found on page 68. | **Hemerocallis** (*Day Lily*). *See* page 79.

Heuchera sanguinea.   *Inula glandulosa.* See page 34.

Hesperaloe Engelmanni, long glaucous green leaves, somewhat resembling a *Yucca.* The flowers are produced in branching spikes, 5 to 6 feet in height, of a beautiful deep yellow colour, tipped with orange. This is closely allied to *H. Yuccæfolia,* which flowered with me some years since, and which remained in flower six months. 5s. each.

Heuchera sanguinea. Of all the numerous interesting Perennials that it has been my good fortune to introduce, none have afforded me so much gratification as this. Its dwarf, compact, branching growth, robust constitution, and its florid habit, taken in connection with the matchless and striking colour of the flowers, render it the most important and valuable of my countless importations. Its usual height is about 2ft., but it varies according to soil and situation, and in some localities it forms specimens far superior to any I have yet seen. The flowers are produced in loose graceful spikes, and borne in extravagant abundance; the colour varies from light coral-scarlet (if the term be permissible) to a shade verging closely on crimson, and when seen in full perfection, especially in sunshine, dazzles the eye with its brilliancy. It is very easily grown in almost any soil, a fact which bids well for its future prosperity. Good plants, 9d.; 8s. doz. Stronger, 1s. and 1s. 6d.; 10s. 6d. and 15s. doz. Seed, 1s. per pkt.

Hesperis matronalis alba plena (*The Old Double White Rocket*) is one of our oldest favourites, and should be grown by everyone. It is easily grown, very free blooming; flowers pure white, very double, lasting a long time in perfection. 6d.; 5s. doz.

Hesperis matronalis purpurea plena, equally as valuable in every way, but with deep purple flowers in compact spikes, very similar to a good German Stock. 6d.; 5s. doz.

Hollyhock, a first-class strain. *See* my Florist Flower Catalogue. Seed, 1s. & 2s. 6d. per pkt.

Hypericum Kalmianum, this rare species is one of the finest of this family, forming erect bushes about 2ft. high, bearing numerous lemon-yellow flowers of great size in terminal clusters; extremely pretty. 9d.

Hypericum nepalensis is a slender deciduous shrub, far more elegant than *H. patulum,* and freer blooming; the flowers are of a rich golden-yellow, graceful, profuse flowering, hardy, and a plant that can be grown in any ordinary border, and one I can recommend. 9d.

HYPERICUM MOSERIANUM.
NEW HYBRID ST. JOHN'S WORT. See page 32.

Hypericum Moserianum. I have much pleasure in again calling attention to this beautiful plant, which was offered for the first time last spring. During the past season I have had opportunities of judging of its merits, the plants being stronger, consequently flowered much freer, but I still feel certain it is capable of still further improvement with age. I have had the annexed illustration prepared by one of our most celebrated artists, to enable my patrons to form an idea of its graceful appearance, as I feel sure it will become one of our most popular hardy plants. It is the first known hybrid in this family, and is supposed to be a cross between *H. patulum* and *H. Calycinum*, the common St. John's Wort, partaking of the habit of the former with the flowers of the latter, and from its great beauty and distinctive character will command the attention of every one interested in first-class border plants. As will be seen from the illustration it is exceedingly graceful, producing long slender much-branched stems leafy to the base, and all drooping towards the points apparently from the weight of the flowers and buds, although the flowers face so that none of its beauty is lost. It is marvellously free blooming, of great size, of a rich golden-yellow, which are rendered still more effective by the numerous yellow stamens and crimson anthers. It is perfectly hardy and free growing, forming a bush about 3 feet in height, and when established is one of the most beautiful Hardy Perennials that I have ever had the pleasure of offering. *See* fig., page 33. Fine strong plants, 1s. 6d.; 15s. doz.

Hypericum uralum, another very distinct species and one of the most graceful effective hardy plants we have. It grows about 2ft., bearing numerous yellow flowers of great substance in clusters of 6 to 8 together. Flowering plants, 9d.; 8s. doz.

Iberis corraefolia, the finest of the evergreen Candytufts, growing about 9ins. in height, producing globular umbels of pure white flowers in spring; useful for cutting. 6d.; 5s. doz.

Iberis Garrexiana, forms an evergreen bush about 9ins. in height, covered with large heads of pure white flowers. 6d.; 5s. doz.

Iberis gibraltarica (*true*), the largest and showiest of this genus, but not quite hardy, forming elegant bushes clothed with large compact heads of white flowers slightly tinged rose. 9d.; 8s. doz. Seed, 1s. pkt.

Iberis sempervirens plena (*The Double White Candytuft*), a fine novelty, beautifully figured and described in my Illustrated Catalogue, No. 84. 9d.; 8s. doz.

Incarvillea Olgæ, a beautiful hardy perennial from Turkestan, which has many admirers. It grows 3 to 4 feet high, producing large trumpet-shaped flowers 2 inches in length, of a bright rose color, inside red; it is of a vigorous constitution, and succeeds in almost any soil, a warm sheltered situation perhaps suiting it best. 3s. 6d. each.

Iris, for full collection, *see* pages 51 to 57.

Inula glandulosa, notwithstanding its introduction in 1840, this noble species is comparatively a stranger in British gardens. It is a native of the Caucasian Alps, and is a Prince among its kind; its large golden flowers, 4ins. across, are wonderfully effective and are admired by everyone. The figure (*see* page 32) gives a good idea of its habit, formation of flowers, &c., and I can strongly recommend it as a really first-class perennial. 1s. each; 10s. doz.

Inula grandiflora, another grand addition to our hardy border perennials, and one that will become a great favourite when better known. In habit is similar to preceding but totally distinct in growth and character, having larger flowers, greater substance, and more rigid; of a rich deep orange colour. It grows about 2ft., stems very stout and erect, perfectly hardy, and will grow in almost any soil or situation; for cutting purposes it will be eagerly sought after, and I would strongly recommend everyone to secure it at once, as the supply is not only very limited but very difficult to replace. Strong plants 3s. 6d. ea., smaller 2s. 6d. ea.

Jeffersonia diphylla, this pretty Berberidaceous plant is now seldom seen, although it is one of the most attractive of Spring flowering plants. The leaves are a beautiful glaucous green with abundance of large pure white flowers; a fine plant for a moist border. 1s. 6d. each.

Lathyrus grandiflorus. But few persons have any conception of the beauty of the Everlasting Peas, or of their great value for cutting purposes. The plate was made from an individual plant in one of my borders; its erect habit is caused by a stick in the centre, without which it would have been more procumbent. It is a fine plant for covering old roots, on the rockery, for filling odd corners where scarcely any other plant would grow, or in the border. The flowers are produced in pairs and are of a bright crimson. *See* fig. page 35. Strong, 1s.

Lathyrus latifolius (*The Perennial Pea*), one of the most useful hardy plants for cutting purposes; flowers large, bright red, and produced in great abundance. 1s. Seed 3d. pkt.

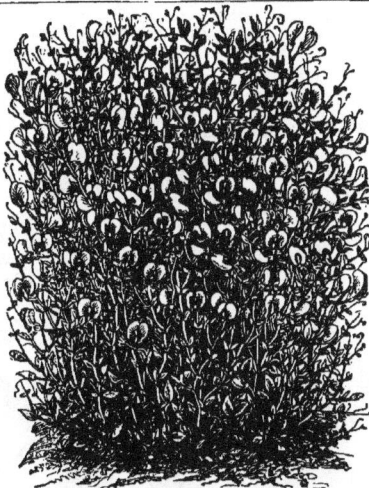

Lathyrus grandiflorus. See page 34. *Lychnis Haageana.* See page 36.

Lewisia rediviva, a marvellously beautiful plant, and one of great interest; leaves linear, clustered, deciduous; flowers of a beautiful satiny-rose, but varying in different specimens. The plant is very persistent, dried specimens having been found to grow after years of mummification, hence its specific name—"rediviva." It succeeds best in a hot dry position, is hardy, perennial, and easily grown. 2s. 6d. each.

Liatris callilepis, a very showy and distinct species, growing about 3 feet in height, bearing large heads of showy pale purple flowers. 1s. each.

Liatris cylindracea. Another species having dense heads of bright purple flowers, a very desirable plant. 1s. 6d. each.

Liatris pycnostachya. This curious old plant, if not entirely lost to English gardens, is so rare that I doubt if any collections exist containing it. The flower stem is simple, and crowded with lovely brilliant rose-purple blossoms. 1s. 6d. each.

Liatris spicata, stem simple, rising erect from a corm or tuber, densely crowded with handsome rose-purple flowers; first-rate border plant, 2 to 3ft. high. 6d. & 9d.; 5s. & 8s. doz. Seed, 6d.

NOTE.—Bees are exceedingly fond of this family.

Liliums. In pots, *see* pages 64 to 66. Full collection, *see* my A B C Guide.

Linaria Macedonica (*new*), producing glaucous leafy stems 2 feet in height, bearing endless spikes of golden-yellow flowers, with an orange lip somewhat resembling a *Snapdragon*; a very striking and characteristic plant, quite hardy, thriving in almost any soil or situation, and grows vigorously. 1s. each.

Linaria pallida, prostrate masses of deep green leaves, covered with violet-purple flowers, lasting in bloom the whole of summer; a fine plant for covering bare banks, rocks, &c. 6d.

Linnæa borealis, a charming little evergreen shrub with slender trailing stems, bearing numerous bell-shaped flowers, in pairs, of a soft rose-colour. 1s.

Linum arboreum, a neat evergreen shrub, about 1 foot in height, leaves glaucous, with large corymbs of bright yellow flowers; a really first-class border or rock plant, and very useful for pot culture, continuing in blossom all through summer. 1s.; 9s. doz.

Linum flavum "luteum." I have every confidence in recommending this invaluable border, rock, or bedding plant; it forms neat symmetrical bushes a foot in height, covered for at least two months with innumerable golden-yellow flowers. A true perennial, hardy, and not the least fastidious as to soil or situation. 9d.; 7s. 6d. doz. Seed, 3d. pkt.

C 2

Lithospermum graminifolium, a pretty ornamental shrub, with graceful grass-like foliage and branching stems bearing clusters of rich deep blue flowers; a perfect gem, but unfortunately very scarce. Was awarded a First-class Certificate by R.H.S. Strong established plants, 3/6.

Lithospermum prostratum, a dwarf evergreen shrub 4ins. high, with brilliant blue flowers in spring. 6d.; 5s. doz.

Lobelia cardinalis, and other varieties. *See* my Florists' Flower Catalogue.

Lobelia syphilitica, a free-growing species, 2ft. in height, flowers light blue, forming a long leafy raceme; a fine plant for a damp shady situation, especially near water. 9d.

Lobelia syphilitica alba, similar to preceding, but with pure white flowers, very showy and distinct. 1s.

Lychnis alpina, producing numerous heads of bright rose coloured flowers, on stems 2ins. high; very showy and distinct. 6d.; 5s. doz. Seed, 6d. pkt.

Lychnis chalcedonica fl. pl., a fine perennial, producing immense heads of vermilion-scarlet flowers, far exceeding in brilliancy many of the double Geraniums; a gem for cutting, and one of the showiest border plants in cultivation. 1s.; 10s. doz.

Lychnis chalcedonica alba pl., the same in every respect as the preceding, but the flowers are pure white; both are perfectly hardy and very free growing. 1s. 6d.

Lychnis dioica rubra fl. pl., very handsome border plant, blooming from early Spring till late Summer, producing myriads of double crimson flowers. Strong plants, 9d.; 6s. doz.

Lychnis flos cuculi alba plena, a double variety of the old "Ragged Robbin"

Lychnis viscaria splendens plena.

perennial; hardy, easily grown, producing myriads of snow-white flowers, beautifully fringed. A gem for the border, the rockery, for exhibition or for cutting purposes. 1s.; 10s. 6d. doz.

Lychnis flos cuculi plenissima semperflorens, a very pretty plant with a very long name, although reduced (without the raiser's permission), and feel certain there must be a still further reduction. It is a double rose variety of one of our wild British plants, growing about 18 inches in height, and producing throughout the summer myriads of double rose flowers beautifully fringed; it is a counterpart of the white one, and will, I have no doubt, become quite as popular. It is hardy, easily grown, adapted for the border, rockery or in pots, and one I have every confidence in recommending. 2s. 6d. each.

Lychnis Haageana, a very showy perennial, about 1ft. in height, remarkable for its striking flowers, nearly 2ins. across, of every shade of colour, from brilliant scarlet to pure white; hardy and easily grown. Mixed varieties, 6d.; 5s. doz. Seed, 3d. packet. *See* fig. page 35.

      6 distinct vars., including white, crimson, rose, scarlet, brick red, &c., for 4s.

Lychnis viscaria splendens plena. Of the numerous red or crimson flowered forms of *Lychnis*, this is considered by every authority to be the finest. It is a variety of the old *L. viscaria plena*, but is totally distinct in colour from that plant. The flowers are large and perfectly double, of a deep scarlet, verging on crimson, and closely arranged on erect wiry stems, much after the fashion of a model Stock. It is perfectly hardy, free blooming, and one of the most useful perennials in my collection; one of the first and foremost plants in existence for cutting or border decoration, and one of the easiest to grow. Strong plants, 9d.; 8s dz.

Lychnis vespertina fl. pl. (dioica alba plena) (*The double white Campion*). Although an old variety of one of our British plants, yet is remarkably rare. When established it forms a pyramid of branching stems 3 feet in height, bearing from June to September, innumerable flowers as large as a crown piece, exceedingly double, pure white and fragrant, somewhat resembling a monster white Pink. For cut flowers it is invaluable, and fine for exhibition purposes. Strong plants, 1s. 6d.

Lysimachia Clethroides, a showy and ornamental perennial, producing numerous stems, 2½ feet, bearing racemes of pure white flowers. Recommended for shady situations. 6d. each.

Lysimachia numularia aurea, this pretty little plant still retains its popularity with all lovers of hardy foliage plants; useful for baskets, pots, or on the rockwork. 6d.; 5s. doz.

Lythrum roseum superbum, a vigorous perennial, about 3 feet, with branching spikes of bright rose-coloured flowers. It thrives in a damp situation, and is very useful for cutting. 9d. ea. Seed, 3d. pkt.

Lupinus arboreus, a very showy and distinct evergreen shrub, producing numerous terminal racemes of bright yellow fragrant flowers. An invaluable plant for a warm sheltered spot in the shrubbery borders, or for planting against a wall where it can be trained like an ordinary climber. 1s. each. Seed, 6d. pkt.

Nirembergia rivularis, see page 38.

Lupinus Nootkatensis, a rare Lupin, 18 inches high; flowers dark blue. 9d.; 8s. doz. Seed, 6d.

Lupinus polyphyllus alba, the white perennial Lupin, bold showy plant. 6d.; 5s. dz. Seed, 3d.

Malva moschata alba, this handsome Musk-scented Malva merits every commendation. Its flowers are very large, of good substance, and a beautiful pure white, and the habit is free and robust. 6d.; 5s. doz. Seed, 3d. packet.

Matricaria grandiflora plena. First Class Certificate. The flowers of this variety are not only much larger than the ordinary variety, but when fully developed are pure white, whereas the original one is more or less greenish in the centre. The plant is dwarf and compact, and has proved a useful plant for bedding and cutting. 9d. each; 8s. doz.

Megasea (Saxifraga). Far too little attention has been paid to this group, which, I think, is owing to the fact that the improved varieties introduced during the past ten years are not known, Amongst spring flowers they stand pre-eminent; hardy, easily grown, evergreen, very free flowering, producing bold massive spikes of many shades and wonderfully effective in the very early spring months. They are also very useful for growing in pots, for a cool house, and can be forced, and will grow well in confined or smoky districts. In the London parks and other open spaces they are among the most conspicuous; and on the Thames Embankment there are scores of huge masses of the older varieties that have been there for years producing marvellous quantities of bloom every season.

Megasea cordifolia purpurea, a very beautiful variety having large massive leathery foliage and bold spikes of rich purple flowers, one of the best of this genus, and one that should be extensively grown in every garden, especially for spring decoration. Strong plants, 9d.

Megasea ciliata, foliage large and hairy, lying close on the ground, flowers white, requiring a somewhat protected situation. 1s. & 1s. 6d. each.

Megasea cordifolia, foliage very large, spikes of bright rose flowers. 9d.; 8s. doz.

Megasea ligulata speciosa, large massive foliage, 12 to 18ins. in length, and bold spikes of rich purple flowers; remarkably free blooming, quite distinct, and one that should be found in every collection. Strong plants, 1s. each; 10s. doz.

Megasea orbicularis, thick leathery foliage, and large heads of rose-coloured flowers. 9d.

Megasea Stracheyi, by far the most beautiful of the Himalayan species. The flowers are large pure white, with rosy-pink sepals, and deep salmon "eyes." 1s. 6d.

Six of the above kinds for 4s. 6d.; two of each for 7s. 6d.

Mertensia virginica, a pretty species, exceedingly effective, stems 18 inches, terminating with clusters of long tubular rich purplish-blue flowers. 1s.; 10s. 6d. doz.

Molospermum cicutarium, a handsome foliage plant, quite as graceful as the *Maidenhair Fern;* very useful for large decorations. 9d. each.

Monardia didyma (*Bergamot*), erect stems 3ft., flowers in whorls of bright scarlet. 6d.; 5s. doz.

Morina longifolia, a distinct and effective perennial, forming rosettes of large deep green spiny foliage and stout spikes, composed of numerous whorls of rose-coloured flowers, white in the bud, closely set in the axils of the leaves. 9d.; 8s. doz. Seed, 3d. pkt.

Myosotis compacta aurea, 6d.; 5s. doz. Seed, 6d. pkt. | **Myosotis elegantissima,** 6d.; 5s. doz.

Myosotis dissitiflora. The finest of the perennial species for massing for spring bedding, flowers light-blue and very free. 6d.; 5s. doz. Seed, 1s. pkt.

Myosotis palustris semperflorens, a perpetual flowering *Forget-me-not,* flowers azure-blue, larger than the type, continuing in bloom until late autumn. A plant I can highly recommend for a damp situation, or even the margin of water. 6d.; 5s. doz. Seed, 6d. per pkt.

Nirembergia rivularis, a dwarf plant with slender creeping stems, forming a thick carpet of foliage, covered during summer with large erect flowers of a creamy-white colour. 1s.; 10s. 6d. doz. *See* fig., page 37.

Œnothera acaulis "Vera." a neat alpine species, forming dwarf cæspitose tufts of greyish foliage and abundance of large white flowers; distinct from all others of this genus. 9d.; 8s. doz.

Œnothera fruticosa major, very ornamental and a great favourite, only growing 2 feet high, smothered with large deep yellow flowers; a first-class border plant. 6d.; 5s. doz.

Œnothera macrocarpa, a good perennial, forming a compact trailing mass, covered with large deep yellow flowers; will grow in almost any soil or situation. 6d.; 5s. doz. Seed, 3d. pkt.

Œnothera riparia, showy species about 1 foot high, composed of a number of slender branching stems, drooping almost to the ground, producing an abundance of showy yellow flowers. 9d.; 8s. doz.

Œnothera speciosa, a free-growing hardy perennial, 2 feet in height, forming tufts of erect stems, covered from June to October with large white fragrant flowers, 2 to 3 inches in diameter. It can be used for bedding, for which it is well adapted, but as a border plant few can be found to equal it. 9d.; 8s. doz.

Œnothera Youngi. One of the best of the Evening Primroses, flowers bright yellow, and very free-flowering. 9d.; 8s. doz.

Œnothera Youngi plena, a double variety of one of the most decorative of our border plants, flowers of a rich golden yellow with several rows of petals, a great beauty and the forerunner of a new race; stock limited. 2s. 6d. each.

Ononis rotundifolia, a neat shrubby perennial, forming a bush 18 inches, producing numerous bright rose flowers; a very characteristic and pretty plant. 9d.; 8s. doz. Seed, 3d. pkt.

Orobus aurantiacus (luteus), a very scarce species, growing 2 to 3 feet high, forming an elegant bush, clothed to the ground with large light green foliage, and bunches of bright orange flowers; a very distinct and beautiful perennial. 1s. 6d.

Orobus lathyroides, a pretty erect perennial, 2½ feet, producing in early summer numerous spikes of small blue flowers, closely arranged; very showy and ornamental. 9d. Seed, 3d. pkt.

Orobus varius. I can still offer this rare and beautiful species, so distinct from all others of this genus, and so remarkably beautiful as to command the attention of everyone. It is erect in habit, remarkably free-blooming, and the flowers of a peculiar shade of salmon and red; it is quite hardy and does well in any ordinary border. 2s. 6d. each.

Orobus vernus purpureus. One of the prettiest of our spring-flowering perennials, forming a bush 1 foot in height, of delicate light green foliage and abundance of deep purple Pea-shaped flowers. 1s. each. Seed, 3d. pkt.

Ourisia coccinea, a handsome plant, having stems 9 inches in height, bearing panicled clusters of scarlet flowers; for a shady border, one of the prettiest plants in my collection. 1s.

Pæonies, Tree and Herbaceous, both single and double. *See* my Pæony Catalogue.

Pansies, Bedding, Tufted, Show, and Fancy. For complete collection, *see* my Florists' Flower Catalogue.

Papavers, a fine collection of new and choice varieties. *See* pages 67 & 68.

Pentstemon. For other varieties, *see* my Florist Flower Cat.

Pentstemon barbatus Torreyi, a tall growing handsome North American plant, often attaining an elevation of 4 feet, forming charming graceful spikes of brilliant scarlet flowers. 6d.; 5s. doz. Seed, 6d.

Pentstemon glaber, a lovely species, about 1 foot in height, producing in early summer long terminal racemes of large flowers, varying from light to dark blue. 9d.; 8s. doz. Seed 3d.

Pentstemon heterophyllus, this resembles in general appearance *P. Jeffrayanus,* forming close tufts of lanceolate foliage and leafy spikes of charming sky-blue flowers. 9d. Seed, 6d.

Pentstemon ovatus, a first-class border plant, 2 feet in height, flowers large, rich blue, on long spikes. 9d.

Physalis Alkekengi.

Phlox, dwarf Alpine species, *see* page 80. For tall varieties, *see* my Florist Catalogue.

Physostegia virginicum. *See* Dracocephalum.

Phygelius capensis, a very effective hardy autumn-flowering plant, growing from 1½ to 3 feet, having pyramidal spikes of long tubular flowers of a rich vermilion with a white throat. 1s.

Physalis Alkekengi (*Winter Cherry*), a very effective hardy perennial, bearing curious white flowers, succeeded by numerous bright red berries, which are most attractive in late autumn, and very desirable when cut for indoor decoration. 6d.; 5s. doz. Seed, 3d.

Pinks, a fine collection of show varieties will be found in my new Florists' Flower Catalogue.

Pinguicula "Butterworts," a charming group of small plants for growing in damp shady spots, will grow on the margins of running streams; flowers rich purple.

Pinguicula alpina, 1s. | **Pinguicula grandiflora,** 1s. | **Pinguicula longifolia,** 1s.

Pityrospermum acerinum, pretty erect slender spikes of feathery white flowers, about 3 feet in height, late in autumn; very effective and useful for cutting. 1s.

Platycodon. *See* Campanula, page 18.

Plumbago Larpentæ (**Valoradia plumbaginoides**), a pretty autumn flowering plant forming a prostrate tuft, composed of numerous wiry stems, from 6 to 8 inches in height, clothed from top to bottom with light green leaves; the flowers are produced in close terminal heads of a rich cobalt blue, in September, lasting until cut off by the frost. 9d.

Podophyllum peltatum, an American species, having large white flowers like a single Camellia, producing pale yellow fruit, about the size of a Plum, beneath the leaves. From the roots of this is obtained the popular medicine *Podophyllin.* Pretty for any damp shady position. Plants, 9d.; 8s. doz.

Podophyllum Emodi, a very curious Himalayan plant, growing about 1 foot in height, with pale green marbled leaves, bearing curious white flowers 1 to 1½ inches across. The fruit is very large and edible, of a bright coral red; it is well adapted for the margins of Rhodo-dendron beds, growing luxuriantly in any damp shady position. 2s. each.

Polemonium humile, flowers pale blue, remarkably free flowering, and only growing a few inches in height. 1s. 6d. each.

Polemonium himalaicum, a charming novelty introduced a few years since, which is not only one of the finest of this family, but a most valuable acquisition to our list of choice peren-nials. It forms large tufts of graceful Fern-like foliage not more than 2 feet high, producing large branching spikes of beautiful azure-blue flowers, 1 to 1½ inches across. It flowers in June and July, and I have much pleasure in being able to offer it, feeling sure it will meet with universal approbation. It was fully described in *The Garden* and *Gardeners' Chronicle.* Strong flowering plants, 9d.; 8s. doz.

Polemonium reptans, a little known, but very beautiful hardy perennial, closely allied to *P. Richardsoni*, but totally different in aspect to any other member of the genus; the flowers are arranged in panicles, and of a lovely shade of blue. 6d. ; 5s. doz.

Polemonium Richardsoni, a really charming perennial from Arctic America, consequently quite hardy; thriving in any soil or situation, exceedingly decorative, and should be universally cultivated. Flowers lovely sky-blue, anthers golden-yellow, forming a charming contrast. Height 1 to 1½ feet, flowers from May to September. Strong plants, 9d.; 8s. doz. Was awarded a First-class Certificate.

Polemonium Richardsoni alba, a white flowering variety, very distinct and pretty, quite distinct from *P. cæruleum album.* 1s. each.

Polygonatum, a very interesting genus of Liliaceous plants, commonly known as *Solomon's Seal.* They are quite hardy, will grow freely in any soil, wet or dry, sun or shade, and are exceedingly ornamental either in foliage or flower, and even after the foliage is decayed the black and scarlet berries of some have an effective appearance. They are very

Ramondia pyrenaica alba.

pretty in pots, are easily forced, and from their beauty deserve more attention than they have hitherto received. They are very distinct in foliage or flower, some producing the flowers in large terminal heads, while others from the axils of the leaves as in the ordinary variety. Many varieties at 6d. each; 4s. dozen. Names on application.

Polygonum cuspidatum, a gigantic-growing plant, 8 feet in height, with large handsome foliage and innumerable white Spiræa-like flowers in the axils of the leaves; very useful for the wild garden, shrubbery borders, or isolated positions on the lawns, &c. 9d.; 8s. doz.

Polygonum japonicum, a dwarf free-growing species, flowers white, in great profusion. 1s.

Polygonum sachaliense, a gigantic growing perennial with tall stout stems, and slightly drooping foliage, having white flowers in axillary clusters; a remarkable plant of quite a sub-tropical appearance, and very useful for margins of waters, shrubbery borders, &c. 1s.

Potentilla formosa, a beautiful old plant, flowering all through the summer, producing myriads of bright cherry-red flowers. 6d.; 5s. doz. Seed, 3d.

Primulas, *see* Pæony and Primula Catalogue, issued with this Edition.

Pyrethrums and Potentillas, *see* my Florists' Flower Catalogue.

Pyrethrum uliginosum, *see Chrysanthemums, page 22.*

Ramondia pyrenaica, a charming little alpine, easily grown, perfectly hardy, and exceedingly interesting when in bloom. The flowers are of a pretty violet-purple, with a bright orange eye. It grows freely in any shady damp spot, and is easily cultivated in pots. 9d. & 1s.

Ramondia pyrenaica alba. Most lovers of alpine plants know the charming Pyrenean Ramondia, which enlivens the shady nooks of our rock gardens with its lovely blue flowers in early spring. But how many of us have seen the first and foremost among the real gems of the Alpine Flora *Ramondia pyrenaica alba,* which I can again offer this season in fine condition. In habit it resembles *Ramondia pyrenaica,* grasping the rocks with its thick leathery Borage-like leaves, and forming compact masses, from which spring a profusion of flowers of a white so pure that it may well dispute the palm of purity with the snow that caps its native Alps. It is easily grown in any damp shady nook in gritty peat. A beautiful plate appeared in the *Garden,* March 7th, 1885, to which I would refer my readers for full particulars of the genus. *See* fig. above. 5s. and 7s. 6d. each.

Ranunculus aconitifolius plenus. *Rudbeckia Newmanni.* See page 42.

See page 42.

Ramondia Heldreichi *(Jankiae)*, long known to Botanists, and eagerly sought for by Nursery-men and amateurs; the actual introduction, however, in a living state has only recently been accomplished. In common appearance it strongly resembles *Ramondia pyrenaica*, but the leaves are hoary and thickly covered with a long silky white pubescens, which considerably enhances the beauty of the plant; the flowers are also borne in a similar manner, only the colour is much more delicate, and the species altogether more beautiful. 5s. and 7s. 6d. each.

Ranunculus aconitifolius plenus *(Fair Maids of France)*, one of the best of our hardy perennials, flowers pure white and exceedingly double, not unlike a miniature double white Camellia. It forms a branching bush 2 feet in height, producing flowers in the wildest profusion which are very useful for cut purposes. It grows freely, preferring a moist shady situation. 9d.; 8s. doz. *See* fig. above.

Ranunculus acris pl. *(The Old Double Yellow Bachelor's Button)*. 6d.; 5s. doz.

Ranunculus amplexicaulis. A very effective plant, and one that can be highly recommended, having flowers as large as a florin, pure white with yellow stamens. Without a question it is one of the very best of our spring flowers, and very useful for cutting purposes. 6d. and 9d.; 5s. and 8s. doz.

Ranunculus Parnassifolius, an extremely rare plant; leaves round, nestling on the ground; flowers large, pure white, four to six on a spike. 1s. 6d. each.

Ranunculus rutæfolius, foliage delicate, deeply divided; flowers large and pure white, 6 inches high. 1s. 6d.

Ranunculus speciosus, immense double yellow flowers, a first-class ornamental perennial for a damp spot. This I can specially recommend. 9d.; 8s. doz.

Ranunculus Thora, a very characteristic plant, forming tufts of glaucous leaves resting on the ground, and large golden-yellow flowers, 4 to 6 inches in height. 9d. each.

Rheum officinale, a plant of gigantic dimensions and very ornamental in foliage and general aspect; the leaves are lobed, very large, measuring 2 to 4 feet across, with branching stems 8 to 15 feet in height. This is the plant from which the "officinale drug" is obtained. 1s. and 1s. 6d.; 10s. 6d. and 15s. doz

Saxifraga Burseriana. From The Garden.

Rheum palmatum, another noble species growing 6 to 8 feet in height, having large foliage divided into narrow segments ; fine for single specimens on lawn, or planted in conspicuous positions among shrubs, where it soon forms an attractive object. 1s. each.

Rhexia virginica (*Meadow Beauty*), a singularly beautiful and remarkable plant. It has a tuberous root, deciduous, with opposite lanceolate leaves, growing about twelve inches high, crowned with numerous bright rosy-purple flowers, and long protruding anthers. It succeeds best in a cool shady border, in sandy peat or leaf mould. 1s. each ; 10s. 6d. doz.

Romneya Coulteri. I can still offer a few of this beautiful plant, at 3s. 6d. each.

Rudbeckia maxima. This genus is one of the most useful of the perennial Composites, the flowers of some being so well adapted for cutting purposes, and all exceedingly free-flowering. This species is one of the largest, growing at least 7 feet high, having large ovate-oblong leaves and yellow flowers, 4 inches across, with a black disc. Strong plants, 1s.

Rudbeckia Newmanni, one of the best of our border plants, producing its showy golden-yellow flowers with jet black centres in great profusion during the autumn, so numerous as to form complete bouquets, in fact there is nothing at that season which produces such an effect. It is largely grown for market, as the flowers are highly appreciated for cutting purposes. *See* fig. page 41. Strong, 6d. ; 5s. doz.

Salvias. These will be found fully described in my *Dahlia Catalogue*, published in April.

Saxifraga Burseriana, the earliest and one of the most beautiful of this group, producing, in the open air in February, large pure white flowers, on scarlet stalks 2 to 3 inches high, the bud before expansion brick-red ; the plant forms compact silvery tufts, which, when covered with flowers, form a very attractive object. It requires a warm situation in comparatively dry soil. *See* fig. above. 1s. 6d. & 2s. 6d.

Saxifraga Fortunei. For elegance and delicacy of structure this rivals the *Gillenia*. The flowers rise in panicles from large light green cordate leaves, each flower representing a star of purest white, and either taken as pot plant or planted in a group it is unequalled in its elegant outline, out-rivalling the finest forms of *S. pyramidalis* in gracefulness. 1s.

Saxifraga granulata fl. pl., a double variety of the common *Meadow Saxifrage*, grows freely in any moist shady border, forming one of the prettiest objects imaginable, having branching stems supporting large double white flowers. 9d.

Saxifraga Wallacei. From "Gardening Illustrated."

Saxifraga Composi (*Wallace*), one of the most valuable and effective hardy spring and early summer bedding plants in cultivation, whether regarded for the striking purity of its white flowers, or for its long-continued bloom and dwarf compact habit. It is unquestionably the best, and no species of the genus can vie with its large white flowers, its deep green mossy foliage; above all, in its unequalled adaptation for massing, edging, or bedding, retaining its verdant beauty undiminished for a very long period. It is also a charming rock plant, and can be used with advantage for cutting. Fine strong plants, 6d. ; 5s. doz.

Saxifraga lantoscana superba, in some particulars resembles *S. longifolia*, but forming large compact masses of rosettes, from which issue innumerable arching feathery-like panicles of the purest white blossoms. It is very superior to the type, and as a rock plant stands alone in this family, and can be most successfully grown in pots. 1s. 6d. ; 15s. doz.

Saxifraga longifolia, immense rosettes 8 to 12 inches in diameter, composed of long silvery leaves margined with white, giving it a frosted appearance. From the centre arises a pyramidal plume 18 inches high, bearing innumerable white flowers; it grows best in perpendicular crevices in rocks; one of the most beautiful of this genus, and has been designated by one of our popular writers as the "Queen of the Saxifragas." 1s. & 1s. 6d.

Saxifraga pyramidalis. This charming old plant is still one of the most beautiful and desirable plants, either for pot culture or the rock garden. It forms large rosettes, from which issue gigantic pyramidal plumes of flowers resembling a cloud of foam, often 3 feet in height, constituting one of the grandest of this genus, and has no equal in its season. Largely grown for Covent Garden, and is one of the great attractions. 9d.; 8s. doz.

Saxifrages.—I have a very rich collection of this family, but only have described a few of the best. A more detailed list may be had upon application. **12 distinct incrusted vars., 6s. and 9s.**

12 mossy kinds, 4s. & 6s.

Scabiosa graminifolia, a distinct species with long silvery foliage and pale blue flowers. 9d.

Scabiosa caucasica. Extract from *Garden,* Sept. 24th, 1881.—"This is one of the handsomest hardy perennials we possess, and one which should be grown by everyone, if only for the sake of its flowers for cutting, a use to which they are particularly well adapted. They last a long time in water, and their peculiar soft lilac-blue shade is charming. It is a plant that stands almost alone in its beauty and character. Flowering plants, 9d. ; 8s. doz. Seed, 6d.

Scabiosa caucasica.

Scolymus grandiflorus, a beautiful Spanish Thistle, forming erect rigid tufts, covered with glistening golden-yellow flowers; a very effective perennial, and distinct in character from any other plant. 1s.

Scoliopus Bigelowi, a most remarkable early spring-flowering plant, and exceedingly rare, closely allied to the *Trilliums,* habit short, with lanceolate deep green leaves spotted with purple like an Orchis, and erect Sea-green flowers spotted green and purple. It grows freely in any half-shady place, in leaf mould or peat, flowering in February. 2s. 6d. each.

Senecio japonicus *(Erythrochæta palmatifida),* an ornamental plant, growing about 4ft., bearing panicles of golden-yellow flowers. The leaves are very large, distinctly palmate, on petioles 3ft. in length. It is hardy, and well worth growing; would look well in large masses. 1s. 6d.

Senecio Doronicum, a free-growing border plant, with large golden-yellow flowers on stems 12 inches in height; a first-class decorative plant, and fine for cutting. 6d.; 5s. doz.

Senecio pulcher, a fine perennial, hardy, easily grown and exceedingly effective, producing large purplish-crimson flowers with a yellow centre, in immense heads on stout stems, 3 feet high; one of the finest of all our autumn-flowering perennials, and a plant that should be found in every garden. *See* fig., page 45. 9d. ; 8s. doz.

Sedum, a pretty group of dwarf growing plants, consisting of a large number of very distinct vars., exceedingly varied in character, some admirably adapted for edging, massing, the rockery, &c. ; others make pretty border plants, and some even adapted for pots. I shall be happy to make selections for any of the above purposes, or to give names, &c.

6 distinct vars., 3s. ; 12 distinct vars., 6s. and 8s.

Sempervivum, "House-leek," a large group of plants exceedingly varied in form and flower, and containing some of the most interesting of the "Alpine Flora." All are hardy, and easily grown on the rockery, while many are invaluable for edging purposes.

6 distinct varieties, my selection, 3s.   12 distinct varieties, 6s. and 8s.

Shortia galacifolia. For historical reasons alone this is the most interesting plant ever offered by me. Discovered by Michaux, more than 100 years since, in the mountains of Carolina, it was described by the lamented Asa Gray more than 50 years ago from imperfect material in the Paris Herbarium, transmitted by Michaux. Till quite recently it had never been met with again. It is a dwarf plant with a creeping root-stock, from which issue numerous fine rootlets, and tufts of long-stalked, evergreen, roundish leaves, the flowers terminating leafless stalks, exceeding in height the tuft of leaves. The flowers are somewhat bell-shaped, over an inch in diameter, pure white, shading into rose as they wither. Its deep bronzy crimson foliage in late summer and autumn, and its exquisitely beautiful pearly white blossoms in spring, render it the most valuable plant ever introduced from the American Continent. Has been awarded highest honours by the Horticultural Society. A beautiful Illustration appeared in my Catalogue last spring. Good plants, 2s. 6d. and 3s. 6d. each.

Sidalcea candida, a pretty Malvaceous plant, growing 2½ ft., having pure white flowers about an inch across closely arranged on the upper portion of the stems. It prefers a moist loamy soil, is quite hardy, an abundant bloomer, and a plant I can recommend. 9d.; 8s. doz. Seed, 6d. packet.

Silene acaulis alba, an indigenous species of great beauty, forming Moss-like tufts of the brightest green verdure imaginable, and pure white flowers set in the foliage. 9d.; 8s. doz.

Silene alpestris, a charming evergreen rock or border plant, forming tufts of dark green foliage, covered with panicles of glistening white flowers; fine for massing. 6d.; 5s. doz. Seed, 3d. packet.

Silene maritima fl. pl., protrate tufts of glaucous foliage an inch in height, bearing double flowers as large as the old "Double White Pink"; remarkably free blooming, and in perfection for months as a rock plant or for the front row of the border, one of the very cream of my collection. 9d.; 8s. doz.

Senecio pulcher, see page 44.

Silene Virginica, attaining in light sandy loam 12 to 18ins. in height; the flowers are few, but very large, of an intense crimson colour, not unlike some of the high coloured varieties of *Lychnis Haageana.* It is quite hardy, easily grown, and one of the most conspicuous rock plants in cultivation. Was awarded a First-class Certificate by the R.H.S. 1/-; 10/6 dz.

Sisyrinchium grandiflorum, composed of tufts of long Grass-like foliage, bearing handsome pendant rich purple flowers in February, frequently in the snow, simultaneously with *Iris reticulata* and *Primula nivalis;* one of the best spring flowering plants. 9d.; 8s. doz.

Sisyrinchium grandiflorum album, this closely resembles the preceding, but the flowers are of a pure satiny-white, and as hardy as it is beautiful. 1s.; 10s. 6d. doz.

Soldanella, a charming little group, forming masses of dark green leathery foliage, and stems supporting several drooping bell-shaped purple flowers, beautifully fringed, giving it a most graceful appearance, requiring a moist shady situation.

Soldanella alpina, flowers deep purple, bell-shaped, and beautifully fringed, leaves small and round, growing up to the snow line, and even blooming through the melting snow. 9d.

Soldanella montana, resembling "*alpina*," but nearly double the size, with a more robust constitution. 1s.

Spigelia marylandica, a plant of much interest and great beauty, forming tufts of slender stems 12 inches in height, supporting numerous tubular flowers from 1 to 1½ inches in length, externally crimson, interior yellow; a damp shady position in peaty soil. 1s. each.

Sparaxis pulcherrima. No other herbaceous plant can compare with this; it is lovely in the extreme, and an adequate description is utterly impossible. It has a charming grace and refinement particularly its own that is matchless in any other plant. It forms long grass-like foliage, 2½ to 3 feet in height, drooping towards their points; from the centre issue the flower-stems, attaining from 3 to 4 feet in height, very slender and wiry, and issuing from the upper portion, say for 2 feet, a number of long wire-like stalks terminating with flowers, varying from crimson to a delicate pink or rose colour, each measuring from 1½ to 2 inches in length, and borne in prodigal profusion. It flourishes in a good rich sandy loam, and in a sunny, moderately dry aspect. *See* fig. of flower. Good plants, 1s. 6d. and 2s. 6d.

Spiræa Aruncus, a noble border perennial, growing 3 to 5 feet high, producing in summer long feathery panicles of innumerable white flowers, forming a graceful gigantic plume. For woodland walks, association with vigorous herbaceous plants, it is unequalled by any perennial in my collection, and is as valuable for forcing as it is for border decoration. 9d. and 1s. Seed, 3d. pkt.

Spiræa Astilboides. The genus Spiræa includes some of the most popular and important border and forcing plants, equally valuable for decorative purposes, or for furnishing cut flowers, while for market purposes they form one of the staple plants of the flower trade. This plant has proved to be a far greater acquisition than was at first supposed, and is without question a grand addition to our list of hardy perennials. It is of the easiest culture,

Sparaxis pulcherrima.

and a most abundant bloomer, growing to the height of 2 feet, succeeding best in a moist situation, and adapted either for the border or for forcing, forming a pretty bush, above which the dense plumes of feathery white flowers are gracefully elevated. The flower plumes differ notably from those of any other species in the purity of the flowers. Was awarded a First-class Certificate. Strong plants, 1s. 6d. and 2s. 6d. each.

Spiræa filipendula pleno, numerous corymbs of double white flowers, surmounting a prostrate mass of delicate pretty Fern-like foliage. One of the best, most useful, and easiest grown perennials in my collection. 6d. to 1s.; 5s. to 9s. doz.

Spiræa japonica aurea reticulata, beautiful green foliage, elegantly veined with yellow. 1s. and 1s. 6d.

Spiræa palmata (*The Crimson Japanese Meadow-Sweet*), a grand border or pot plant, producing large heads of crimson flowers and handsome light green foliage, and growing luxuriantly in any ordinary border. 6d. and 9d.

Spiræa palmata alba, a pure white variety, similar in habit, adaptabilities, &c., to the old *palmata*, a really beautiful decorative plant; has been awarded two First-class Certificates. *Garden*, Sep. 4th.—"This plant is likely to become as popular as the type, especially as it has proved to be amenable to forcing." Again *The Garden* says: "A snow-white variety having large spreading plumes, without a trace of colour in them, &c. 1s. and 1s. 6d.

Spiræa palmata elegans, intermediate in colour between the crimson and white variety. 6d. &9d.

6 distinct varieties for 3/6.

Statice Gmelini, a strong growing variety, producing immense branching heads of small dark blue flowers. This is one of the best of the family and should be in every garden. 9d.; 8s. doz.

Statice latifolia (*Great Sea Lavender*). The value of this as a decorative plant is now recognized by all lovers of hardy plants, and it is equally well-known that, like many others, it varies considerably from seed, and some forms are worthless. The one now offered is the true form, a variety that has never been surpassed, and at present is the most valuable acquisition in the genus. It forms heads 2 to 3 feet across composed of dark blue flowers; invaluable for cutting, for winter decoration, the flowers, when dried, lasting for months. 9d.; 8s¹ doz. Seed 3d.

Statice Limonium, large heads of deep blue flowers quite distinct in character from any others of this group. 9d.; 8s. doz. Seed, 3d.

3 distinct varieties for 2s.

Stokesia cyanea, a first-class perennial, growing 2 feet in height, bearing a profusion of lavender-blue flowers 3 inches across. This plant flowers very late in autumn, consequently should be planted in a warm sheltered situation, or could be lifted and placed in the conservatory, where it will flower till Christmas. 9d. and 1s.

Symphytum officinale argenteum variegatum, a very bold and handsome foliage plant, producing leaves of great size, of a deep green, having a broad bold margin of silver at the edge of each leaf. 9d.; 8s. dz.

Symphytum officinale aureum variegatum, similar to preceding, but with leaves larger and margined with a bright golden-yellow. 9d.; 8s. doz.

Thalictrum anemonoides, elegant Fern-like foliage, and pure white flowers nearly an inch across, on stems 3 to 4 inches high; a pretty plant for a shady peat border or rockwork. 9d.

Thalictrum adiantifolium (*The Maidenhair Thalictrum*), a beautiful plant, rivalling the *Maiden-hair Fern* in the delicacy of its foliage, but hardy and easily grown in any ordinary border, and an invaluable plant for bouquets. 9d. Seed, 3d.

Thermopsis montana, a pretty perennial from California; flower-stems erect, 2½ to 3 ft. in height, terminating with racemes of large yellow Pea-shaped flowers, and a remarkably free grower. 1s.

Tiarella cordifolia (*Foam Flower*), a plant of great beauty both in leaf and flower, perfectly hardy, easily increased, and flourishing in almost any soil and position. The single blossoms are small, of a creamy-white colour, and star shape, the buds before expansion delicately tinged with pink. The flower stems are well above the foliage and densely crowded with feathery white blossoms, in the distance resembling "foam," hence the common name. Whether in rock, garden, or border, it is a beautiful and effective plant, and one I can thoroughly recommend. 6d. and 9d.; 5s. and 8s. doz.

Trollius Fortunei plena.

Tradescantia virginica, a showy and highly decorative group of border plants for naturalizing in shrubbery borders, woodland walks, &c. They form erect bushes 18 ins. in height, producing numerous terminal umbels of large flowers, which are produced in great profusion the whole of the summer. There are several varieties—white, red, double red, rose, light blue, and deep violet, can supply collections as under:

6 distinct varieties for 3s.; 12 in 6 varieties for 5s.

Trilliums, for full Collection *see* page 78. | **Tritomas**, for full Collection *see* page 79.

Trollius, this is one of the greatest favourites of our Spring flowers. The whole of the varieties are vigorous growers, large handsome foliage, forming bold subjects. They are all remarkably free flowering, flowers large, bright clear colours; and for cutting purposes or for general decoration are indispensable. They luxuriate in swampy situations, fond of shade, and in such spots form masses, which, when covered with flowers, form glorious objects, and no garden should be without them. The following are the best:

Trollius Fortunei plena, a very fine form of *Trollius asiaticus*, having dark green foliage and rich bronzy stems smothered with large semi-double orange flowers; for decoration or for cutting in the early spring months, one of the best flowering plants in my collection. 1/6 each.

Tropæolum polyphyllum.

Trollius Loddigesianus, a very fine form of *Trollius europæus,* with large globular flowers of a pale yellow. 9d.; 8s. doz.

Trollius, mixed varieties, these are mixed varieties, varying all more or less in size of flower, and shade of colour, running through various shades of orange, lemon, and yellow; fine for naturalizing, or massing in the borders. 6d.; 5s. doz. Seed, 1s. pkt.

Tropæolum pentaphyllum, a vigorous climber, bearing scarlet flowers, tipped green, a rapid grower, and quite hardy when thoroughly established, requiring a deep rich alluvial soil. 1/6

Tropæolum polyphyllum, a grand decorative trailing plant, graceful glaucous foliage and abundance of golden-yellow flowers in long tresses, completely covering the ground, hardy, easily grown, and a great favourite with every one, and propagates rapidly, increasing in beauty every season. 9d.

Tropæolum speciosum, one of the choicest hardy climbers in existence, producing a blaze of scarlet flowers in late summer and autumn. This is the plant seen so much in Scotland, covering the houses with sheets of bloom during late summer and autumn. It grows rapidly, preferring a light alluvial soil, and in a somewhat shaded situation. 1s. Seed, 1s.

Tropæolum tricolor (*Jaratti*), a vigorous greenhouse climber; flowers scarlet, green, and yellow; a gem when well grown in pots. 1s. 6d.

Tropæolum tuberosum, an extremely handsome climbing species, producing in great profusion red and yellow flowers, and growing about 8 feet in height. 3d.; 2s. 6d. doz.

Tussilago fragrans (*The Winter Heliotrope*), flowers in mid-winter, and very fragrant. 6d.; 5s. dz.

Uvularia grandiflora, a pretty plant, closely allied to the *Solomon's Seal,* forming tufts of slender stems about 12 inches in height, producing an abundance of long drooping yellow flowers from the axils of the leaves, quite hardy, growing freely in any shady border. 1s.

Veratrum nigrum, a noble and stately plant, distinct in character from any other, and wherever planted forms a conspicuous object. It grows about 5 feet in height, producing stout rigid stems and immense plicate leaves, the lower ones recurving, the upper horizontal. The flowers are about the size of a sixpence, of a rich bronzy black, arranged in a large branching head, and grows freely in any soil or situation. A plant I cannot too highly recommend, especially for planting in masses. Strong plants, 1s. each.

Tradescantia Virginica. See page 47.   *Veronica longifolia subsessilis.*

Veratrum album lobelianum, somewhat similar in general appearance, but with greenish white flowers. 1s. each; 10s. 6d. doz.

Verbascum olympicum, a very remarkable and showy species, having large white silvery foliage, surmounted by a pyramid of golden yellow flowers. 1s.

Verbascum phœniceum, a group of effective free growing perennials, producing innumerable erect spikes 2 feet in height, thickly set with white, purple, rose, and red flowers. 6d.; 5/- dz.

Verbena venosa, a showy perennial, growing from 12 to 18 inches in height, and producing from June until late in the Autumn, a profusion of bluish violet flowers; a very effective plant for Summer bedding, and a great favourite in the London Parks. 6d.; 5s. doz.

Veronica longifolia v. subsessilis, a Japanese variety, of great merit, and is decidedly the best of this family, and one of the most handsome perennials in cultivation, wonderfully free blooming, flowers rich purplish blue, in large massive spikes, both flowers and spikes much larger than any of this genus, and grows luxuriantly in almost any soil or situation. 9d.; extra strong, 1s. *See* fig. above.

Veronicas. I have many other varieties in my collection, either for rockwork or border. **6 distinct varieties for 3s. 6d.; 12 distinct varieties for 6s. and 8s.**

Viola pedata, a most charming American species. Leaves pale green, deeply divided; flowers of the loveliest mauve-blue. It should be planted on the rockery in sandy loam, and partially shaded and moist.

Viola pedata alba, rare, 2s. 6d. each. | **Viola pedata bicolor,** 1s. each.

Xerophyllum asphodeloides (*Nutt*), a very interesting and pretty plant, with long, rigid, narrow evergreen leaves, a foot or more in length, reclining somewhat in the way of *Asphodelus luteus.* From the centre rises a spike of showy white flowers, thickly beset with needle-shaped leaves, shortening until the summit is reached, when they assume bristle-like bracts. 1s. 6d.

Yuccas, a good collection of hardy varieties; names, sizes, and prices on application.

Zauschneria californica, one of the best autumn flowering perennials, 18ins. in height, flowers bright vermilion, in loose one-sided spikes, which, from its brilliant colour and great profusion, forms an attractive object. It grows best in a dry situation, in loamy soil, and is quite hardy. 9d.; 8s. doz. Seed, 1s. 6d. pkt. *Salvia clivulis.*

Zauschneria californica splendens, quite distinct, the flowers of an intense vermilion, quite an acquisition to our list of autumn-flowering perennials. 9d.

N.B.—Rockeries and Ferneries made or re-modelled, and Landscape work undertaken by a competent staff.

D

New Hybrid Tritoma (Kniphofia.)

(Red-hot Poker).

A stately genus of Liliaceous plants, forming tufts of long, broad, fleshy, grass-like leaves, from which are thrown up numerous stout stems, bearing spikes of scarlet and yellow flowers, commonly known as "Red-hot Poker," "Flame Flower," or "Torch Plant." There are many species which are exceedingly handsome and well worth cultivating, especially some of the new kinds now offered. They will grow in almost any soil or situation; most of them are hardy, and those which are not, are easily protected by a slight covering during severe weather. They are invaluable late in the Autumn, when the majority of border plants have been marred by the early frosts, which, however, has no influence on the Tritomas, as they continue to flower late in the Autumn. They are seen to the best advantage at the back of the mixed border, in large clumps among shrubs, dotted here and there on the lawn, in conspicuous positions on the rockery and many other places, while the dwarf growing ones are charming for forcing in pots.

Tritoma (Kniphofia).

Burchelli, an early flowering robust species, flowering usually in August. The flowers are dark red, passing to orange, large spikes on stems 2 feet in height. 9d.

caulescens, a rare arborescent species, having long, broad, glaucous blue foliage and massive spikes, 5 to 6 feet, of brilliant flowers, upper portion bright crimson, lower bright yellow. 2/6 and 3/6 each.

corallina, a sterling novelty, one of the most showy of the dwarf growing varieties. It grows about 2ft. high with bright green foliage, and heads of brilliant scarlet, shading into orange red, and remarkably free flowering, somewhat similar to *T. Macowani.* Strong plants, 1s. 6d.

H. Cannell, immense long spikes 4 feet high, bearing plumes 9 to 12 inches long, composed of long narrow petals of a bright coral red, keeping the colour even when fading. 5s. each.

Leichtlini, a grand species from Abyssinia, growing from 3 to 4 feet high, of a close compact habit, bearing immense plumes of a glowing yellow, with protruding red stamens, forming a striking contrast. 2s. 6d. each.

Leichtlini aurea, distinct from all, immense massive heads of bright orange flowers. 2s. 6d.

Leichtlini Distachya, long protruding anthers, bright scarlet and yellow flowers, one of the most distinct and effective of this group. 3s. 6d. each.

Nobilis, the grandest of the group, immense spikes of orange-red flowers on stems 6 to 7 feet, blooming from August to December. 2s. 6d. each.

Otto Mann, an exceedingly free flowering variety, with large spikes of pale orange flowers, changing to deep orange. 3s. 6d. each.

O. Späth, a very fine and very effectual variety, spikes of bright coppery-red, changing to bright red, very free and robust habit. 5s. each.

Pfitzeri, a very pretty new variety which will be serviceable, owing to the flowers being of a pure bright crimson colour, without a tinge of orange or yellow seen in so many other varieties; in shape it is similar to *T. Macowani,* in fact, it might be mistaken for a very large dark variety of it. It is thoroughly hardy, and a really first-class variety. Nice plants, 3s. 6d.

Uvaria, spikes of scarlet flowers shading to orange, in August, about 3 feet. 9d.; 8s. doz.

Uvaria aurea, this is an exceedingly free flowering variety, plumes large, of a bright orange colour, very distinct. 1s.; 10/6 doz.

Uvaria glaucescens, large spikes of vermilion-scarlet fls., shading to orange after expansion. 1s.

Uvaria grandiflora, splendid spikes of rich crimson and orange flowers, one of the last in bloom. 1s.

Victor Lemoine, long dense spikes, petals very broad, of a tawny orange colour, shading to vermilion, 4 feet high, very distinct. 3s. 6d.

IRIS.

Probably the most Complete Collection in existence.

For many years past this family has been one of my great specialities, and has the reputation of being one of the most complete collections in existence. Many may have seen my annual displays at the Spring Exhibitions in May, June, and July, which have invariably received highest honors. Thousands of spikes are cut for this purpose, and when mingled with Pæonies, Lilies, Pyrethrums, and other hardy flowers, form a display of unparalleled beauty, and attract more attention than any other group in the Exhibition. I have flowered a large number of new varieties of *Iris Kæmpferi*, both single and double, some measuring 8 to 9 inches across, and quite new in colour; every shade can be found in this gorgeous group, which is destined to become one of the most popular sections of this family. Of the *Germanica* or *Flag Iris*, I think I may say my collection is "unique," there is not a bad variety enumerated. I have been working at them for years, raising numbers of new varieties, which have proved vast improvements upon the old varieties.

As the collection of Iris is so large, and their adaptabilities for various soils and situations so varied, I shall be happy to make selections for hot dry soils, heavy wet soils, water, spring flowering, rockwork, or for general decorative purposes, in any soil or situation.

German Iris (Iris Germanica).

This group includes all the broad leaved Iris, which generally pass under the above name, but are really varieties of *pallida, neglecta, squalens, amœna, variegata, aphylla,* and *germanica,* all resembling each other in foliage and habit, but totally distinct in flower; taken as a whole, they form a group unparalleled in beauty, nothing in creation can vie with them, unless it is the Orchids from the Tropics. Every shade of colour may be found among them, and as they will thrive in almost any soil or situation without any care whatever, they must be considered necessary in every garden. For the Wild Garden, Shrubbery Borders, Margins of Water, Rockwork, &c., they are admirably adapted; in fact, hardly any place can be found in which some of this section will not thrive. The whole of the following are first class varieties, including many novelties of my own raising, which I now offer with the greatest assurance that they will give satisfaction; they are good strong plants, and can be highly recommended.

My selection, carefully selected, so as to thoroughly represent the group, as under :—

	s.	d.		s.	d.
12 good selected varieties for	6	0	12 extra fine varieties for	8	0
25 in 12 good selected varieties for	11	0	25 in 12 extra fine varieties for	15	0
50 in 12 good selected varieties for	20	0	50 in 12 extra fine varieties for	27	0
100 in 12 good selected varieties for	37	6	100 in 12 extra fine varieties for	50	0
100 in 25 good selected varieties for	55	0	100 in 50 extra fine varieties for	60	0

Fine mixed varieties, per doz. 3s. 6d.; per 100, 25s. Those not priced, 9d.; 8s. per doz.

D 2

GERMAN IRIS
GRACCHUS.

GERMAN IRIS MADAME CHEREAU.

Awarded First-Class Certificate.

From the "Journal of Horticulture."

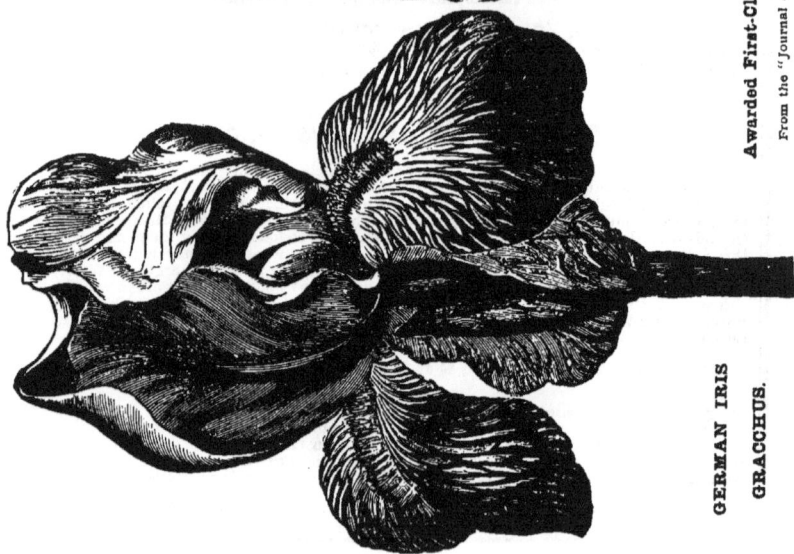

GERMAN IRIS—*continued.*—Those not priced 9d.; 8s. per doz.

Action, (S) yellow, (F) deep crimson, conspicuously veined with white. 1s.
Albicans (*Prince of Wales*), (S & F) pure white, the largest and purest in colour of this group.
Arnold, (S) bronze-violet, (F) rich purple, reticulated white and orange.
Atropurpurea, (S & F) rich purple, very free, and very early flowering. 6d.
Aurea, (S & F) golden-yellow, a fine bold flower, and the finest of all yellows. 1s. 6d.
Bridesmaid, (S) pale lavender, (F) white, reticulated lavender, very fine. 1s.
Calypso, (S & F), pale blue, veined white and pale lilac.
Celeste, (S & F) deep lavender, very large and free-flowering with conspicuous orange-beard.
Cordelia, (S) rosy lilac, (F) deep purplish-crimson, margined and tinted white.
Cytheree, (S) lavender, (F) purple veined white, a very attractive and taking flower.
Darius, (S) chrome yellow, (F) purple, margined pale yellow and reticulated white, a very distinct
    and remarkable variety. 1s. 6d.
Dr. Bernice, (S) brown, (F) purple, reticulated orange and white.
Donna Maria, (S) white, (F) white shaded lilac, a great favourite.
Duchesse de Nemours, (S) pale lilac, (F) purplish violet, veined and margined white.
Eclipse du Soleil, (S) pale yellow shaded with bronze, (F) coppery, with a distinct yellow margin,
    a very conspicuous variety.
Flavescens, (S & F) light primrose yellow, very large, fine flower, and remarkably free blooming.
Florentina, (S & F) white, very free-flowering and sweet scented. 6d. each; 5s. doz.; 25s. 100.
Garibaldi, (S) pale yellow and bronze, (F) brownish purple. 2s.
Germanica, (type), (S) purplish-blue, (F) purple. 6d.; 5s. doz.; 25s. 100.
Gracchus, (S) lemon, (F) pale yellow, reticulated purple, dwarf compact growing, remarkably
    free-flowering, is admitted by all to be one of the finest varieties ever raised (was awarded a
    First-class Certificate by the R. H. S.). 1s.; 10s. doz.
Hector, (S) yellow, (F) brownish red stained purple.
Hericart de Thury, (S) chrome-yellow, (F) plum-coloured, reticulated sulphur and white.
Lucretia, (S) purplish bronze, (F) lavender, shaded with purple.
L'Innocence, (S) pure white, (F) white, slightly veined orange, a very fine form. 1s. each.
Mme. Chereau, (S & F) white, edged and feathered violet, and pale blue, very free. 1s.; 9s. dz.
Madame Paquette, (S) purplish-red, (F) rosy purple, a very fine form. 1s.
Madame Patti (*new*), (S & F) rosy-purple, shaded bronze, very fine. 1s. 6d.
Magnet, (S) bright yellow, (F) purple, reticulated white.
Maori King, a beautiful seedling variety, having the (S) golden yellow, (F) deep velvety crimson. 2s.
Mr. Gladstone (*new*), (S) lilac feathered white, (F) deep blue, robust grower and very free. 2s. 6d.
Othello, (S & F) deep purplish-blue, a most intense rich shade.
Pallida Dalmatica, (S) lavender, (F) lavender tinged purple, flowers very fine and large. 2s. 6d.
Pallida concolor, (S & F) lavender, well shaped flower. 1s.
Pallida Mandraliscæ, a very rare species, somewhat in the way of *I. germanica*, of remarkably
    compact growth, and numerous deep blue flowers. 1s. 6d.
Pallida racemosa, (S) deep lavender, (F) lavender, very early and free flowering, very fine. 1s.
Pallida speciosa, (S & F) purplish violet, very distinct, robust and free flowering, one of the best.
Pallida propendens, (S & F) deep lavender, very large, tall, handsome variety. 1s.
Penelope, (S & F) white, veined reddish violet.
Plumeri, (S & F) deep coppery red, very early and free flowering. 1s.
Poiteau, (S) white, tinged lavender, (F) deep purple, reticulated white, very large flower. 1s.
Portia, (S & F) white and lilac, edged and veined violet, very fine. 2s. 6d.
Queen of May, (S) rosy lilac, (F) rosy lilac, veined yellow, a very fine and distinct form. 1s.
Rigolette, (S) golden yellow, (F) deep crimson purple, a very fine free-blooming variety. 1s. 6d.
Socrates, (S & F) bronze, shaded and feathered lilac-purple. 1s.
Spectabilis, (S & F) deep purple, very early and free flowering.
Tinææ, (S & F) deep blue, shaded lilac, fine large flower. 1s. each; 10s. 6d. doz.
Ulysses, (S) golden yellow, veined white, (F) yellow veined and reticulated white.
Victorine, (S) white, blotched purplish blue, (F) violet purple, veined white. One of the most
    beautiful of this family; was awarded a First-class Certificate by the R.H.S. 1s. 6d.
Victor Hugo, (S) golden yellow, (F) deep crimson, veined bright yellow, very fine. 2s.
Wallneriana, (S) coppery shaded, bluish violet, (F) yellow, shaded with blue.

One of each of the above 50 extra fine varieties, the finest in cultivation, for 42s.

Japanese Iris *(Iris Kœmpferi or lœvigata).*

A new group of Japan Iris, totally distinct in flower from all others of this genus. They form strong tufts of lovely bright green foliage from 3 to 4 feet in height, surmounted by large Clematis-like flowers both single and double, some of immense size, from 6 to 10 inches across, of almost every shade of colour—red, white, blue, rose, crimson and purple, striped, splashed, and veined in the most exquisite manner. They prefer sunny moist situations, by the side of ponds, streams, etc., planted in loam, where they soon become established, and form striking and very ornamental objects. The following are the very best varieties in cultivation; the colours of many are entirely new, and the flowers larger than anything yet raised.

Alexander von Humboldt, single, snow-white flowers, veined yellow. 1s. each; 10s. doz.

Anne Boleyn, large double deep purple blue flowers tinted crimson-purple. 2s. 6d.

Bismark, double, large violet-purple, tinted blue, compact habit. 2s. 6d. each.

Cassandra, flowers double, deep lilac, passing to white and violet, very fine. 2s. 6d. each.

Cleopatra, large double, deep violet, passing to blue. 2s. 6d. each.

Dante, large, deep bluish-purple flowers, veined lilac, very double. 2s. 6d. each.

Elizabeth, large, single, white rosy-lilac centre, compact habit, very fine. 2s. 6d. each.

Excelsior, double, large deep plum coloured flowers, yellow centre, surrounded with white. 2s. 6d.

Flora, double large deep blue, tinted violet-purple, very robust and free. 3s. 6d. each.

Helene von Siebold, flowers large, single, pale rose coloured, very free. 1/6; 15/- doz.

Jersey Belle, flowers large, perfect, double pure white, symmetrically shaped. The best of the double whites, and one of the best Iris for cutting. 2s. each; 21s. doz.

Kæmpferi (*lœvigata*), rich violet flowers, very robust. 6d.; 5s. doz.

Leonidas, large double flowers of a deep purplish crimson. 2s. 6d.

Lucretia, double large plum-coloured flowers, tinted and shaded white. 2s. 6d.

Macbeth, single, flowers of a soft plum colour, beautifully feathered, white centre. 2s. 6d.

Madame Le Grelle d'Hanis, white rosy centre and tinted pink. 1s.; 10s. doz.

Progress, double, very large, deep crimson, flaked pale lilac. 2s. 6d.

Robin Hood, large double, violet-purple tinted blue, centre purplish blue. 2s. 6d.

Venus, very large, pure white flowers, centre yellow. 2s. 6d.

Souvenir, large bright pink flowers, very double. 2s. 6d.

Iris Kœmpferi vars.

Mixed Seedlings, single and double, a fine strain, 9s. doz; 65s. per 100.

IMPORTED VARIETIES DIRECT FROM JAPAN.

This is a magnificent lot selected from some of the best collections in Japan, and contain varieties of marvellous beauty, of immense size, both single and double; in some colours quite new to this group. These are one year established, and offered just as received, without any good varieties being selected from them, and every plant may be relied upon as being quite equal to the best named varieties. 18s. doz.

COLLECTIONS OF IRIS KÆMPFERI.

12 distinct varieties, 18s. and 24s. per doz.; 24 in 12 varieties for 30s. and 36s.

Older kinds, 12 distinct varieties for 12s. All of these are offered in exceptionally strong stuff.

Iris, Miscellaneous Species & Vars.

Among these will be found some of the most interesting of this family, exceedingly varied in size, habit, adaptabilities, &c., collected from all corners of the earth. Many of them are totally distinct from the ordinary *Flag;* in some, the flowers are simply immense and the most grotesque combinations of colour; while others are remarkably small, forming masses of foliage, and when in bloom very effective. Among this section are to be found species that can be grown in every conceivable situation and soil, and flowering from Christmas until late Autumn.

In the following descriptions, s *signifies standards, or the erect petals;* F *falls, or lower drooping petals;* ¶ *requiring a warm dry situation;* ‖ *requiring light sandy soil;* * *ordinary soil in the open border;* † *in damp situations, margins of streams;* G *greenhouse, &c.*

‖ **arenaria,** growing about a foot high, with grassy foliage and beautiful golden-yellow flowers, which are produced in great numbers. 2s. each; 20s. doz.

¶ **agrostifolia,** rare species, flowers pale blue, very early. 3s. 6d.

Iris atropurpurea.

* **aurea,** a robust species in the way of *I. ochroleuca,* deep golden-yellow flowers, one of the best of the late-flowering varieties; beautifully figured in the *Garden,* January 15th, 1887. 3s. 6d.

¶ **atropurpurea** (*Baker*), another beautiful species belonging to the Oncocylus section, and allied to *I. iberica* and *I. Susiana.* The foliage is narrow, short, and of a glaucous green; stem about a foot high, bearing one or two flowers of a deep brownish-purple, almost black, and a large black blotch furnished with yellow hairs near the base of the falls. *See* fig. above. Described in *Gardeners' Chronicle,* March, 1889, page 330. Beautifully figured in *Regel's Gartenflora,* December 15th, 1891. Strong plants, in pots, 1s.; 10s. doz.

* **chinensis** (*Pardanthus*), flowers erect, resembling a *Tigridia,* of a brick-red or pale scarlet colour, beautifully marked crimson and white. 1s. each; 9s. doz.

‖ **cristata,** a gem, well adapted for the rockwork and border, flowers numerous, small, pale-blue, hairy and beautifully fringed and crested. 1s.

‖ **Bloudowi,** a very pretty species from Central Asia, growing from 1 to 1½ feet in height, with deep yellow flowers. 2s. each.

† **cuprea,** pretty coppery-red flowers, one of the best of the late-flowering kinds, and almost the only species of this peculiar shade of colour. *See* also *I. fulva.* 1s.; 10s. 6d. doz.

* **ensata var. oxype tala,** an ornamental species from Turkestan, resembling in growth *I. Sibirica;* (s) pale blue; (F) lilac; fully figured and described in *Regel's Gartenflora.* 1s.

* **ensata fragrans,** resembling the above in colour and form, but with sweet-scented flowers, and about a month earlier in bloom. 1s. 6d.

* **ensata var. triflora** (*biglumis*), flowers pale blue, netted white; usually flowering twice during summer. 1s.

* **Fieberi,** (s & F), large, deep purple, tinted violet, very early and free, 9d.; 7s. 6d. doz.

G **fimbriata,** one of the best and most beautiful of the half-hardy Iris, producing its flowers in great abundance during the winter and early spring; at first sight it might be taken for *Vanda cærulea,* the colour and form being somewhat similar; most useful for cutting or for decoration. Strong plants, established in pots, 1s. each.

* **fœtidissima,** an indigenous species with evergreen leaves and purple flowers, succeeded by pods of an antimony-red colour, which are largely used for Christmas decorations. 9d.

* **fœtidissima fol. variegata,** very decorative plant, with white margined foliage. 1s.; 10s. doz.

IRIS, MISCELLANEOUS SPECIES AND VARIETIES – continued.

† **fulva**. This is often considered to be synonymous with *I. cuprea*, they are, however, quite distinct, *I. fulva* flowers much later and with much larger and deeper-coloured flowers, and the foliage broader and longer. 2s. 6d. each.

* **graminea**, (s) erect purple; (F) bright purple, tinted with sky-blue. 9d. ; 7s. 6d. doz.

* **graminea latifolia**, large flowers, produced in clusters of 3 or more, and broader foliage; a very handsome variety. 9d. ; 7s. 6d. doz.

* **Guldenstüdteana**, tall and very robust, its bold massive foliage is yellow during the spring, changing to green in summer, with sulphury flowers. 2/6 each.

¶ **hexagona**, one of the most distinct of this genus, having long evergreen leaves and large sky-blue flowers, the centre of falls bright yellow. 1s. 6d. ; 15s. doz.

* **humilis**, (s) purple-blue; (F) purple, veined with white and tinted blue. 1s. 6d. each ; 15s. doz.

G **ixioides**, foliage arranged in fan-shaped tufts, flowers erect, small white, marked blue; very elegant and showy plant. 1s. 6d.; 15s. doz.

* **longipetala** (*californica*), (s) lavender; (F) very long, of a pale blue, veined white; very free and robust; one of the most characteristic of the group. 1s. ; 10s. doz.

* **longipetala var. compacta**, the whole habit of plant is compact, flowers large pale blue, veined white, and very free-flowering. 1s. 6d. each ; 15s. doz.

Iris Nazarensis (Bismarkiana).

* **longipetala var. minor**, differing from *longipetala*, in having smaller flowers and long narrow leaves of a glaucous green colour. 1s. ; 10s. doz.

* **lutescens**, of dwarf growth, and large bright yellow flowers. 9d. ; 7s. 6d. doz.

¶ **Mariae** (*Helenae*) *new*, another grand addition to the *Oncocyclus* group, its growth and habit resembles *Iris iberica* or "*Susiana*," but the standards are a bright lilac, occasionally veined black; falls of an intense rich velvety-purple veined black, each limb marked with a still deeper blotch of black. It is, perhaps, the most beautiful of this section. Easily grown in a dry sheltered spot in light sandy soil. Strong, in pots, 2s. 6d. ; 24s. doz.

¶ **Milesi**, an Himalayan species of recent introduction, with large well expanded flowers of a beautiful pale lilac-purple, veined white, the centre of the laminæ yellow. 1s. 6d. ; 15s. doz.

* **Missourensis** (*Nutt*), a fine species with long glaucous linear leaves, and pale blue flowers on slender stems, with 2 to 4 flowers on each; a very early flowering variety, and a great favourite; the best for cutting of the early flowering Iris. 1s. 6d. ; 15s. doz.

* **Monieri**, a vigorous species, growing from 4 to 6 feet high, with deep green stiff and erect leaves and large golden yellow flowers, one of the best of this group. 2s.

* **nudicaule**, (s and F) rich purple flowers, very free, one of the best of the late spring flowering Iris; fine for forcing, massing, &c. 6d. ; 4s. doz.

* **ochroleuca**, a noble species, growing from 3 to 4 feet in height, with large white and yellow flowers. 9d. ; 7s. 6d. doz.

† **Pseudo Acorus** (*The common Water Iris*), flowers bright yellow. 6d. ; 4s. doz.

† ———— **fol. var.**, one of the prettiest of Water Flags, leaves broadly margined with yellow. 9d.

* **Redouteana** (*Spach.*), an early free flowering species with dull purple flowers, sweetly scented. 9d

* **ruthenica**, a pretty and distinct species, forming tufts of deep green grassy foliage, and handsome purplish-blue flowers, Violet scented. 2s. each ; 21s. doz.

IRIS, MISCELLANEOUS SPECIES AND VARIETIES—continued.

¶ **Saari var. Nazarensis** (*I. Bismarkiana*). I have succeeded in obtaining a further supply of this rare species, perhaps the most remarkable of this beautiful section. It has a vigorous constitution, and one likely to succeed in our climate. The foliage is erect, of a glaucous green, the flowers very large, similar to *Iris Susiana*, but the standards are light blue, veined with purple, while the falls are of a peculiar ashy grey, beautifully veined with blackish purple, having three large jet black blotches on the falls. It is a very distinct species, and is perhaps the most beautiful of the Holy Land Iris. It requires a light soil in a sunny sheltered spot. Well established plants, in pots, 1s. 6d.; 15s. doz.

¶ **Susiana** (*The large Mourning Iris*), flowers large, (S) black, (F) grey, very large and expanded, veined black, and the centre with a large dark velvety black blotch. Plants in pots, 1s. each.

* **stylosa**, a lovely winter flowering species, having beautiful light blue flowers, with yellow blotches, produced in abundance in January. As it flowers so early the flowers should be protected or planted in a warm sheltered spot; near the sea it does well. 9d. and 1s.

* —— **var. Elisabethæ** (*new*), an exceedingly pretty variety of dwarf growth, leaves narrow, grass-like; flowers large, of a deep blue tinted lilac and white, sweetly scented. 2s; 21s. doz.

* —— **speciosa**, a very fine new variety with rich deep blue flowers, beautifully netted white, much larger than the type, and flowering quite as early. 1s. 6d. each; 15s. doz.

¶ —— **alba**, beautiful pure white flowers during the winter and early spring. Was awarded a First-class Certificate, Spring, 1889. This is a great acquisition, and should be grown wherever a sheltered spot can be found against wall or border. It is quite hardy, but as it flowers so early should be planted in a protected situation. 2s. 6d.; 24s. doz.

¶ **tectorum**, lovely pale blue flowers, blooms early, should be grown under glass or in a very warm spot, as it is scarcely hardy. 1s. 6d.

† **virginica pallida**, (S) violet, (F) purplish-violet, beautifully veined, foliage very elegant. 9d.

† —— **purpurea**, (S) purple, (F) deep purple, veined white. 9d.

* **verna** has a very neat and dwarf habit, having glaucous grass-like foliage 6 inches in length, and large dark violet-blue flowers, Violet scented. It flowers in early spring, and is well adapted for rockwork, the open border, or for pot culture. Strong clumps, 1/6; 15/- doz.

12 distinct varieties of the above for 8s., 12s., 18s., and 24s. doz.

Siberian Iris (*Iris Sibirica*).

A very distinct group of Iris, distinguishable at a glance by their long grassy foliage, 2 to 3 feet in length, forming dense erect tufts, and numerous slender stems, bearing an abundance of flowers of various shades. They are quite hardy, very free growing in any ordinary soil, and invaluable for cutting.

6 distinct varieties for 3s. 6d. | 12 in 6 varieties for 6s. | 50 in 6 varieties for 21s.

Iris Olbiensis.

Another early flowering section of dwarf Iris, closely allied to the Pumila Section. They grow from 9 ins. to 1 ft. in height, immediately succeeding the Pumila Section in time of flowering. The foliage is broader, and the flowers larger, and borne in great profusion. They are also well adapted for early forcing and pot culture. The following are all good distinct varieties.

6 distinct vars. for 3s. | 12 in 6 varieties 5s. | 25 in 6 varieties 9s. | 100 in 6 varieties 32s.

Crimean Iris (*Iris Pumila*).

A charming group of dwarf spring-flowering Iris, growing from 6 to 9ins. in height, producing an abundance of lovely flowers from March to May; they are admirably adapted for the decoration of the border, as edging plants, or for bedding, and as they grow vigorously in any soil, they cannot be too highly recommended for spring decoration. They are, like the *olbiensis*, well adapted for forcing.

12 distinct varieties of the above section for 3s.; | 12 in 6 varieties for 5s. 6d., 32s. per 100.

Ornamental Grasses, Bamboos, &c.

For imparting a tropical effect to the Flower Garden, planting in the centre of beds, on the lawn, or in conspicuous positions in the shrubbery border; also for the "Wild Garden," margins of lakes and streams, for edging, and various other purposes, which the plants themselves will suggest. All are hardy, free-growing, and many of them, especially the Tree Grasses, are among the most conspicuous of our foliage plants. They are well adapted for pot culture, forming fine specimens, and are exceedingly decorative.

Arundo Conspicua, a noble plant for isolated positions on the lawn, &c., forming tufts similar to the *Pampas*. 1s. 6d.

Arundo donax (*The Common Bamboo*), a grand plant for a marshy situation, forming noble clumps 12 to 16 ft. in height. 1/- & 1/6.

Arundo donax variegata. This is a noble and very effective plant, hardy, easily grown, and would form an imposing object in almost any position, especially near water. It is also used for bedding, forming a pretty effect. The foliage is beautifully variegated, and forms an effective object grown in pots for conservatory decoration. Strong plants, 1s. 6d.; extra strong, 2s. 6d.

Bambusa aurea, a very distinct and beautiful species, attaining from 12 to 18 feet in height, the stems are of a rich golden-yellow colour, which blends harmoniously with the light green foliage; one of the finest of the Tree Grasses. 3s. 6d.

Bambusa gracilis, this is one of the most graceful of this family, it is perfectly hardy and wonderfully useful for decorative purposes. I have an exceptionally fine stock, of my own raising, which I can offer at the exceptionally low price of 1/- each, 10/6 doz. for good established plants in pots; a few extra strong plants at 1/6 each, 15/- doz.

Bambusa flexuosa, a new species, producing clumps of long slender canes, which gracefully droop at the points, giving the plant a very elegant appearance. 3s. 6d.

Bambusa Henonis, a new Japanese variety, one of the finest of the hardy varieties ever introduced to this country. It is erect in habit, soon attains a height of 12 to 18 ft., having dark green leaves and stems of a pale sulphur and of a most graceful habit. 5/-

Bambusa metake, a handsome evergreen

Bambusa gracilis.

species of a very vigorous habit, having large deep green foliage; fine for the shrubbery borders, margins of water, &c. Strong plants, 2s. 6d. Specimens, 5s.

Bambusa mitis, among beautiful foliage plants this is a gem. The stems, which attain a great height, are of a pretty lemon-yellow, and clothed with handsome foliage. 3s. 6d.

Bambusa nigra, another handsome species, having glossy black stems with very graceful foliage of a pleasing light green colour, very distinct. 2s. 6d. & 3s. 6d.

Bambusa Quilioi, a new Japanese introduction of a very vigorous habit, growing 8 to 12 feet in height, forming large clumps of pale lemon-yellow stems and foliage; very effective. 5/-

Bambusa Scriptoria, a very rare and distinct species, having slender straw-yellow stems and remarkably fine grass-like foliage. It is quite hardy, growing about 8 feet, and is one of the most elegant. 3s. 6d. each.

Bambusa Simmonsi, one of the most vigorous and rapid growers of this family, canes 10 to 12 feet in height, shooting from the ground in every direction, soon forming impenetrable brakes clothed to the ground with long graceful foliage. 2s. 6d.; 24s. doz.

Bambusa viminalis, a new distinct dwarf-growing species, with dark deep green foliage. 3/6.

Bambusa violascens, another species having much branched stems attaining 7 to 8 feet in height, clothed with very graceful foliage, very handsome and distinct. 3/6.

Bambusa viride glaucescens, a vigorous growing species, very graceful & ornamental stems yellow, foliage glaucous green, in appearance resembling *B. aurea*. 2s. 6d.

Carex japonica variegata, a pretty variegated sedge, fine for pots or for edging purposes. This, and many other of the variegated Grasses force well, and are exceedingly useful for cutting in Spring. 9d.

Carex tenuis fol. variegata, a very ornamental variegated sedge, foliage erect, slighly drooping at the points, every leaf broadly margined with golden-yellow, having a very pleasing appearance and one that will become a favourite for edging purposes, for borders, for rockwork, or grown in pots. 1s. each; 10s. 6d. doz.

Dactylis elegantissima, one of the best of the hardy silver variegated Grasses for edging purposes. 6d. each; 5s. doz.

Dactylis elegantissima aurea, foliage broadly margined with gold; the most effective grass for edging purposes. 6d.; 5/- doz.

Elymus glauca, glaucous blue foliage 4ft., very showy, a grand plant for covers. 6d.; 5/- dz.

Eulalia japonica, a very useful plant for the border. 1s. and 1s. 6d. each.

Eulalia japonica foliis striatus, this has a white band running through the centre of each leaf, giving it a very pleasing appearance. It is quite hardy, and one of the most effective of our grasses. 1/6 & 2/6.

Eulalia zebrina.

Eulalia japonica zebrina, a remarkable variegated plant, having bars of yellow running crossways, not longitudinally as in the ordinary form of variegation; quite hardy, easily grown, and one of the most ornamental grasses in cultivation; *see* fig. 1s. 6d. and 2s. 6d.

Eulalia gracillima, one of the most exquisite grasses yet introduced; so graceful that no words of mine can give any idea of its great beauty. It is similar in growth to the type, forming a clump 3 to 4 feet in height, composed of remarkably fine grass-like foliage, gracefully drooping at the points, giving the plant a most elegant appearance. It is an acquisition for the borders, centre of beds, isolated clumps, or in pots. 2s. 6d. each.

Gymnothrix latifolia, a very ornamental grass, especially for pots. The foliage is broad, very abundant, gracefully drooping at the points, one of the easiest and cheapest decorative plants to grow. It dies down in winter, and breaks up again in spring. 9d. and 1s. each.

Gynerium argenteum (*Pampas Grass*), forms magnificent clumps of graceful foliage, fine for the centre of beds, clumps, on the lawns, &c., the cut plumes are very useful for winter decoration, &c., can be dyed any colour and will last for years. 9d., 1/- to 2/6. Seed, 6d. pkt.

Phalaris elegantissima, fine for shrubbery borders or edging large beds. This is the best of the large variegated grasses for cutting purposes. 6d.; 5s. doz.

Stipa pinnata, the light feathery awns are extensively used for making everlasting bouquets, and is offered for sale in every shade of colour under the name of *Feather Grass*. 6d.; 5s. doz.

6 of the most distinct varieties of Bamboos for 15/-, 18/- and 21/-

Hardy Aquatics.

I am pleased at being able to offer a number of new Water Lilies, and my collection of these is a very unique one. Among the novelties are some very remarkable varieties, quite as beautiful as the Tropical varieties, and almost every shade of colour may now be had among the hardy Water Lilies. Some of the flowers are of immense size, fragrant, with massive foliage of various shades, while in some the foliage is beautifully marbled.

Adapted for planting in streams, lakes, ponds, or in stagnant water from 2 inches to 3 feet deep; all are hardy except those marked *, these are suitable for indoor Aquaria; those marked † are for shallow water, the remainder for deep water.

With a little judgment in selecting, and care in planting, our swamps, ponds, lakes, streams, and even stagnant pools, could be made beautiful by planting suitable subjects, some to cover the surface with foliage and flowers, others rising majestically above them, while the margins should be fringed with pretty flowering plants. The best time for planting is from March till October, but the more common indigenous plants may be planted at any time. The following list embraces the very best adapted for this purpose.

12 distinct varieties, my selection for 8s., 12s., 15s., 18s., and 24s. per doz.
24   ,,   ,,   ,, 20s., 25s., 30s., and 42s.   ,,

†**Acorus Calamus** (*The Sweet Flag*), long green lanceolate foliage, resembling an Iris. 6d.

†**Acorus japonicus argenteus striatus**, a beautiful Japanese plant, having long sword-like foliage beautifully striped red, white and yellow, a really good plant. 1s.; 10s. 6d. doz.

†**Alisma natans**, an effective floating plant with pretty white flowers. 9d. each; 8s. doz.

†**Alisma Plantago**, this bears large panicles of small white flowers. 6d.

***Aponogeton distachyon**, a perfect gem, flowers large, peculiar in formation, white with dark anthers, powerfully scented like Hawthorn, can be grown in or outside, in shallow or deep water. 1s.

†**Brasenia peltata** (*Water Shield*), small coppery peltate foliage floating on the surface, and brownish-purple flowers, a distinct and very pretty plant, adapted for Aquaria. 1s. 6d.

†**Butomus umbellatus** (*The Flowering Rush*), one of the most beautiful of our British plants, flowers numerous, of a bright pink, in large heads, should be grown in every wet place. 9d.

†**Calla palustris** (*Bog Arum*), flowers like a miniature Calla, and quite hardy. 1s.

†**Cyperus longus**, one ot the prettiest of the Sedges, a very useful foliage plant. 6d.

Dulichum spathaceum, a very curious and distinct plant for the margin of water. 1s. 6d.

Hottonia palustris (*Water Violet*), a pretty submerged Fern-like plant with showy white fls. 9d.

Nymphæa odorata.   *Aponogeton Distachyon, see page* 60.

Hydrocharis Morsus Ranæ (*Frog-bit*), native plant, pretty for stagnant pools, can only be supplied from May to Autumn, while in a growing state. 6d.

*Limnocharis Humboldti, a gem, distinct in character from any of our native plants, flowers rich golden-yellow, and beautifully fringed; one of the most exquisite in cultivation. 3/6 each.

†**Menyanthes trifoliata** (*Bog Bean*), a free-growing plant, a gem for growing in very shallow water, mud, &c., flowers white, in spikes much resembling the Horse Chestnut. *See* fig., page 63.

*Myriophyllum proserpinacoides, pretty as a foliage plant, leaves remarkably elegant and graceful. 9d.

Nuphar advena (*The large yellow-striped Water Lily of America*), a very robust species with immense foliage and flowers. 2s. 6d.

Nuphar luteum (*Common yellow Water Lily*). 1s.

Nuphar Kalmianum, a charming plant with cordate light green leaves and yellow flowers, half the size of the common yellow Water Lily, with red carpels, very floriferous, well adapted for in or out-door. 3s. 6d. each.

Nuphar sagittæfolium (*new*). A most interesting and pretty species with long arrow-shaped leaves and pale yellow flowers; very rare. Good flowering plants, 3s. 6d. each ; 36s. doz.

Nymphæa alba (*The Common White Water Lily*). 1s. 6d. each ; 15s. doz. ; smaller, 1s.; 10/6 dz.

Nymphæa alba var. rosea, the Swedish rose-coloured variety, without a doubt one of the loveliest of all the Aquatics, and perfectly hardy; guaranteed the true variety. 30s. each.

Nymphæa candida, an extremely rare plant from Northern Europe; leaves very large, copper-red, and pure white, almost double flowers; habit free and robust. 3/6 each ; 36/- doz.

*Nymphæa flava, a very rare species from the Southern States and one of the best of the genus, flowers large, bright yellow, leaves beautifully marbled with purple, distinct from any other of this genus. 3s. 6d. each.

Nymphæa Marliacae, a new Hybrid Water Lily, one of the finest introductions among aquatics for many years past, having bold marbled foliage, and large canary yellow flowers nearly double, and very hardy and robust. 5s. each.

Nymphæa Marliacae albida (*new*). A vigorous grower, large massive foliage and very large milky white flowers, tinted flesh and pale pink, and exceedingly free flowering. Flowering plants, 7s. 6d. each.

Nymphæa Marliacae carnea (*new*), large beautifully marbled foliage, and flesh-coloured flowers, very robust and free. 10s. each.

Nymphæa odorata. Sweet-scented North American White Water Lily. 1s. 6d. & 2s. 6d.

Nymphæa odorata Exquisite (*new*). Flowers almost double, outer petals of a bright rose colour, centre petals of a delicate pink, very free. 10s. 6d. each.

Nymphæa odorata minor, small flowered form, flowers of exquisite formation, pure white. 2/6

Nymphæa odorata rosea, similar to the type but with large rose-coloured flowers, a great beauty and very rare. Strong plants, 5s. each.

Nymphæa odorata rubra. An American variety of great beauty, hardy and very easily grown; flowers deep rosy red, and very sweet-scented. Strong flowering plants, 7s. 6d. each.

Sagittaria Montevidensis.   *Villarsia Humboldtiana.*

Nymphæa odorata sulphurea, another new hybrid with large sulphur-yellow flowers, powerfully Vanilla-scented, and a very robust grower. Strong plants, 7s. 6d. each.

† **Nymphæa pumila.** A very dwarf American species with small leaves and numerous sweet-scented small white flowers well adapted for small Aquaria. 2s. 6d. each.

† **Nymphæa pygmæa**, a real gem, medium sized marbled foliage and white flowers, exceedingly free, well adapted for in or out doors. 3s. 6d.

† **Nymphæa pygmæa var. helvola**, a new hybrid of very free habit and small sweet-scented flowers of a pale primrose colour, and pretty marbled foliage. 5s. each.

Nymphæa tuberosa, closely allied to *N. odorata*, but much longer leaves and pure white flowers. This forms small tubers. 2s. 6d. each.

Nymphæa Laydekeri rosea (*New Hybrid*), large bright rose carmine flowers and orange stamens, wonderfully effective and having a very robust constitution and quite hardy. A few specimens only of this most remarkable hybrid. 30s. each.

† **Orontium aquaticum** (*Golden Club*), a very characteristic-looking plant, having large bold foliage, and a curious yellow Spadix. Small plants, 1s. each.

† **Peltandra virginica** (*The Water Arum*), large arrow-shaped foliage, white Spadix. 1/6 & 2/6.

✗† **Pontederia cordata**, a charming free-flowering plant, growing about 2 feet high, and producing spikes of closely set blue flowers. 1s. 6d. and 2s 6d.

✗† **Sagittaria sagittifolia** (*The Common Arrow-head*), flowers white with dark-coloured anthers, one of the prettiest of our British water plants. 9d.; 7s. 6d. doz.

✗† **Sagittaria japonica plena**, immense double white flowers, one of the best and most distinct of all the flowering Aquatics; quite hardy and very easily grown. 3s. 6d.

✗† **Sagittaria montevidensis**, this is a grand acquisition to our list of Aquatics, producing large sagittate foliage 2 to 4 feet in height, and spikes of large pure white flowers marked with three maroon spots. Beautifully figured in the *Garden*, page 8, No. 685 (*see* fig. above). 3s. 6d.

✗ **Stratiotes aloides**, has long spiny recurved leaves, and spikes of white flowers, in general appearance resembling a "Pandanus," but growing under the water instead of above, the flowers only being in the air; it is easily grown and a great curiosity. 9d.; 7s. 6d. doz.

† **Typha angustifolia** (*The long-leaved Cat's-tail*). 1s. †T. **latifolia** (*The common Cat's-tail*). 9d.

† **Typha minima** (*The Miniature Cat's-tail*), a very elegant and pretty plant. 1s. 6d.

✗• **Vallisneria spiralis fœmina**, a pretty plant for in-door Aquaria. 1s. 6d.

✗† **Vallisneria spiralis mascula**, similar to above. 1s.

† **Villarsia lacunosa**, round heart-shaped leaves and white flowers; very pretty. 1s. 6d.

† **Villarsia nymphæoides**, a charming little plant, covering the water with circular shining leaves and myriads of yellow Ranunculus-like flowers. 1s.

✗• **Villarsia Humboldtiana**, a very pretty floating species, with light green roundish leaves and pure white flowers most beautifully fringed. 3s. 6d. each. *See* fig. above.

✗ **Villarsia reniformis**, kidney-shaped leaves and yellow flowers, very free flowering. 1s. 6d.

Bog Plants.

SUITABLE FOR THE MARGINS OF WATER, BOGS, DAMP BEDS, etc.

Arundo donax *(The Great Bamboo)*, grows 12 to 18 feet high, a grand plant for a moist spot. 1s. and 1s. 6d.

Bambusa metake, useful in the border and on the margin of streams. 1s. 6d. and 2s. 6d. For full collections of Bamboos, *see* pages 58 and 59.

Caltha palustris *(The Marsh Marigold)*, flowers deep golden-yellow, very early in spring. 6d. ; 5s. doz.

Caltha palustris plena, large double golden-yellow flowers. 9d.; 7s. 6d. doz.

Caltha leptosepala, with large Ranunculus-like white flowers. 1s. 6d.; 15s. doz.

Cardamine trifoliata, a small growing plant, best adapted for very wet places on the rockery. 9d.

Carex atrovirens, a very handsome club-rush, growing 3 feet, having triangular stems and heads of olive-green. 1s. 6d.

Carex hystricina, a curious species, with yellowish flowers. 1/6.

Carex lupuliformis, large handsome spikes, 2 to 3 ft. long. 1s.

Cypripedium pubescens *(The Hoary Lady's Slipper)*, flowers golden-yellow. 1s. 6d. and 2s. 6d.

Cypripedium parviflorum, flowers smaller, rich yellow, pretty in any damp shady spot. 2s.

Cypripedium spectabile, fully described on pages 72 to 75, and also figured. 1s. 6d. and 2s. 6d.

Drosera rotundifolia *(The British Sundew)*, one of the carnivorous plants. 9d.

Gunnera scabra, immense foliage, an imposing subject for the margins of streams, &c. 2s. 6d.

Habenarias, a group of Orchids, admirably adapted for boggy situation. For full description, *see* page 73.

Menyanthes trifoliata.

Iris Kaempferi, in several varieties, *see* page 54.

Iris Pseudo acorus foliis variegatis *(The Yellow Water-Flag)*, with yellow variegated leaves. 9d.

Iris Pseudo acorus pallida, a variety of the Common Water Flag, with pale yellow flowers. 9d.

Juncus conglomeratis fol. var. *(Common Rush)*, beautiful striped golden foliage. 9d.; 7/6 doz.

Juncus Zebrinus. *See* Scirpus.

Myosotis palustris semperflorens *(Perpetual-flowering Water Forget-me-Not)*. 6d.; 5s. doz.

Orchis foliosa *(The Madeira Orchis)*, for description and figure, *see* page 74. 2s. 6d. each.

Osmunda gracilis, the most graceful of this genus, either for pots or planting out. 1/6 & 2/6.

Osmunda regalis *(The Royal Fern)*, in suitable positions this forms gigantic specimens, and is perhaps one of the most effective of all the British Ferns. 1s. and 1s. 6d.

Parnassia caroliniana, 1s. } A pretty group of small-growing Bog Plants. *P. palustris* is
Parnassia fimbriata, 1s.   } known as the *Grass of Parnassus;* all the varieties have white
Parnassia palustris, 9d.   } flowers and reproduce themselves freely, and when seen in masses have a very charming appearance.

Pinguicula grandiflora *(The Irish Butter-wort)*, flowers large, of a light purple colour. 9d.

Pinguicula longifolia, curious long strap-like leaves and rich deep purple flowers. 1s.

Polygonum Sieboldi, a very handsome plant, growing from 6 to 9 feet high, with heart-shaped leaves, and racemes of white flowers. 1s.

Primula rosea, for full description, *see* separate catalogue. 9d.; 8s. per doz.

Sarracenia purpurea *(The Hardy Pitcher Plant)*, for description, *see* page 82. 1s. 6d. & 2s. 6d.

Saxifraga Fortunei, for figure and description, *see* Alphabetical Collection. 1s. each.

Saxifraga peltata, large handsome foliage, quite distinct from any other of this family. 1s.

Scirpus Tabernæmontani, var. Zebrinus, the most elegant of this family, leaves 4 to 6 feet, delicate green, barred alternately with white, should be in a sunny position. 1s. 6d.; 15s. doz.

Spiræas, in variety, for full description of this showy group of Meadow Sweets, *see* Alphabetical Collection. 6d. to 1s. 6d. ; 5s. to 15s. doz.

12 distinct varieties, 6s., 8s., and 12s. | 25 distinct varieties for 14s. and 21s.

Lilies in Pots.

ABRIDGED LIST.

For full description of this family see my Catalogue of Lilies published in Autumn. It contains one of the best collections in existence, all fully described and freely illustrated.

NOTE.—The following is a selection only for Spring planting.

NOTE.—After the middle of March they will be supplied in pots.

12 distinct varieties selected from the following for 9s., 12s , 18s., 24s. & 30s. the dozen.

Auratum (*Yami Yuri of the Japanese*), this is one of the greatest favourites on account of its great beauty, delicious fragrance, abundance of bloom, and the ease with which it can be grown, coupled with the low price at which it is offered. My importations this season are in grand condition, bulbs firm and fresh, and will be sure to flower well. **Fine flowering roots, 9s. and 12s., and very large bulbs 18s. and 24s. doz.**

Auratum platyphyllum, a most lovely variety of *Auratum*, having leaves and flowers from two to three inches larger than the type, the petals overlapping almost to the tips, thus forming an immense flower; the petals too, are much stouter, and the general appearance of the plant marks it at once distinct from any variety in cultivation. 1s. 6d. and 2s. 6d. each; 16s. 6d. and 24s. per doz. A few extra fine bulbs, 36s. per doz.

Auratum rubro-vittatum, one of the most gorgeous Lilies yet introduced, and the most vivid description would fail to give an idea of its beauty. It is a medium growing variety of *Auratum*, with narrow dark green leaves and dark stems, producing immense white flowers with an intense blood crimson band, 1 to 1½ inches in width, running through each petal, giving the flower a most remarkable and brilliant appearance. 3s. 6d. and 5s.

Browni, one of the most beautiful of Lilies, immense trumpet-shaped flowers, 10 inches in length; interior pure white with chocolate-coloured anthers, exterior brownish-purple, tips of the divisions slightly recurved. Strong roots, 3/6, 5s. and 7s. 6d.

Canadense flavum, flowers bell-shaped, soft yellow, thickly spotted with crimson, one of the best and most distinct species for a damp shady spot. 1s.

Canadense rubrum, a most handsome and graceful Lily with bell-shaped flowers of a deep orange scarlet colour spotted brown. 1s. 6d.

Elegans alutaceum, grows about 1 foot in height, with large soft Apricot-coloured flowers, spotted with black; one of the most distinct of this section. 3 bulbs in a pot, 1s. 6d.

L. Browni.

Elegans bicolor, flowers erect and large, of a rich apricot flamed with scarlet. 9d.

Elegans fl. pl., large double flowers of a deep crimson colour. 1s. 6d. each; 15s. doz.

Elegans Prince of Orange, deep apricot-coloured flowers, spotted black, very free. 9d.; 8s. doz.

Elegans sanguineum, large crimson flowers, flaked orange. 3 bulbs in a pot, 1s. 6d.

Elegans Wallacei, glowing apricot, freely spotted with maroon, one of the most beautiful of this group. Awarded a **First-Class Certificate by the R.H.S.** 1s.; 10s. 6d. doz.

Giganteum, the most majestic of all Lilies with large ornamental foliage and long trumpet-shaped flowers, white, often tinted purple and sweetly scented, on stems 8 to 15ft., preferring a half-shady spot in moderately moist light soil. 3s. 6d., 5s., 7s. 6d. and 10s. 6d. each.

Grayi (*new*), of great beauty, with flowers in the way of *canadense*, of deep crimson colour. 5/6 ea.

Hansoni, one of the most beautiful and remarkable of the Martagon section, of very robust and free habit, and with flowers of a deep yellow colour, tinted orange, and spotted maroon, segments very thick, like wax. Strong flowering bulbs, 5s. each.

Humboldti, one of the finest of the Californian Lilies, growing 6 ft in height, producing from 10 to 20 large flowers, of a rich golden-yellow, spotted with crimson purple, while the tip of each segment is of a clear golden yellow (*see* fig. p. 65). 1s. 6d. and 2s. 6d.; 15s and 24s. doz.

LILIES—*continued.*

Humboldti var. Bloomerianum magnificum, one of the most beautiful of the Californian Lilies, and very rare. It is very vigorous, growing 6 to 8 feet, flowers large, and are produced in great abundance, of a deep rich orange-scarlet, shaded purple, and conspicuously stained crimson purple. Extra large bulbs, 7s. 6d. each.

Krameri, lovely in the extreme, slender stems 2 feet in height, surmounted by one or more large flowers of a most beautiful rose colour. It can be grown in pots or planted out on a south border in sandy soil. 1s. & 1s. 6d. each ; 10s. 6d. & 15s. per doz.

Leichtlini, flowers large, bright yellow, spotted with crimson, one of the rarest and most beautiful of autumn-flowering Lilies. 3s. 6d. each ; 36s. doz.

Longiflorum. Extra fine bulbs of this beautiful pure white Lily, 3 bulbs in a pot, 1s. 6d. ; 15s. doz.

Martagon *(Purple Turk's-cap Lily)*, a pretty European species, bearing spikes of purple flowers, and growing from 5 to 8ft., of very easy culture, consequently well adapted for naturalization in woods or the wild garden. 6d. and 9d. ; or three in a pot, 1s. 6d. & 2s. per pot.

Martagon album, pyramidal heads of white flowers, one of the finest of this family. A gem in every respect and easily grown, was awarded a **Floral Certificate.** June 22, 1889. 3s.

Martagon Dalmaticum, the *Dalmatian* form, with twice the number of flowers, of an intense crimson-purple almost black. One of the most beautiful of the European Lilies. 2s. 6d.

Martagon Catanæ, a fine form of Martagon of exceedingly robust growth, often attaining a height of 8 feet with 50 flowers, approaching those of *Dalmaticum* of a deep vinous purple tinted black. 1s. 6d. each.

Monadelphum var. Szovitzianum. A Lily of great beauty, large and attractive, and one of the first in flower. It varies from deep golden-yellow to pale primrose, spotted more or less with black ; the flowers are of great substance, beautifully recurved, and produced freely. Fine roots, 1s. 6d. ; 15s. doz. *See* fig. p. 66.

L. Humboldti.

Odorum (*L. Browni var. Colchesteri*), a very rare and beautiful species, trumpet-shaped flowers, when first opening a pale sulphur changing ultimately to a pure white, exterior striped brown and purple, very sweetly-scented, well adapted for the open border in light soil and a splendid pot plant. Large flowering bulbs, 5s. each ; 48s. doz.

Pardalinum, bright scarlet shading to orange, and freely spotted with maroon ; flowers large, from 6 to 12 upon a stem, 6 to 7 feet in height. 1s. and 1s. 6d.

Pardalinum Bourgaei, one of the best and most distinct of this group, growing about 6 to 7 feet with beautiful large flowers of a deep crimson, tinted orange and spotted maroon. 2s. ; 21s. doz.

Pardalinum Michauxi, a late flowering variety with numerous scarlet flowers tinted deep yellow and spotted maroon. 2s. each ; 20s. doz.

Parryi, bright yellow flowers, spotted with maroon, and very sweet, distinct in form from any other Lily, and is one of the most beautiful species in cultivation, especially for a damp spot. 3s. 6d. and 5s.

Pomponium (verum). This is very early, and grows about 3 feet in height, bearing numbers of fiery scarlet flowers, not unlike the old *Scarlet Martagon*, but far more graceful ; one of the most beautiful of all known Lilies ; was figured in the *Garden*, 1881. *See* fig., page 66. 9d ; 7s. 6d. doz.

Pyrenaicum, large yellow flowers spotted black, one of the earliest. 9d.

Rubescens (*true*), one of the most distinct and beautiful of the Californian Lilies with medium sized erect flowers of great substance, at first they are ivory white spotted crimson, changing the second or third day to a beautiful lilac-purple and sweetly scented. 3s. 6d. each.

Speciosum (lancifolium of some). This is a large group of autumn-flowering plants, containing a great number of magnificent varieties, all of which are adapted for pots as well as the open border. They are all quite hardy, very free blooming, and will succeed in any ordinary border.

E

LILIES—*continued.*

Speciosum album, flowers large white, exterior tinted rosy purple.   1s. ; 10s. 6d. doz.

Speciosum album monstrosum, with fasciated stem and medium sized white flowers, which are produced in the greatest profusion, a strong bulb often bears more than 50 flowers. 9d. ; 7s. 6d. doz.

speciosum album Krœtzeri, immense white flowers of great substance, with a greenish band running through the centre of each petal; one of the finest.   1s. 3d. ; 12s. doz.

speciosum album verum, flowers large, pure white, with yellow stamens, the earliest and one of the best of this group. Extra large bulbs in pots, 2s. 6d. each ; 24s. doz.

speciosum album punctatum, pure white, faintly spotted and shaded with delicate pink spots, a distinct and pretty variety.   1s. 6d. ; 15s. doz.

speciosum purpureum, large red flowers, tinted purple, and heavily studded with dark crimson-purple spots. One of the most effective of the whole of this group. 1s. ; 10s. 6d. doz.

speciosum purpureum Melpomene, deep purple flowers, heavily tinted with deep crimson, and margined white. A very fine variety. 1s. 6d. each; 18s. doz.

speciosum roseum, pale rose flowers, tinted deep rose, very free. 9d.; 7s. 6d. doz.

superbum, a grand and beautiful Lily, with deep orange, tinted yellow and crimson, and spotted maroon flowers, fond of a light spongy soil, rather damp and shady. 9d.; 8s. doz.

tenuifolium, one of the most elegant and beautiful of the early flowering dwarf Lilies, fiery scarlet flowers, 10 to 20, on stems 1 to 2ft. high; a gem for pot culture. Flowering roots, 1s. & 1s. 6d.

L. pomponium (see page 65).

testaceum, one of the most beautiful and distinct, with large nankeen coloured flowers, easily grown in almost any soil or situation. Well adapted for town gardens. 1s. 6d. ; 15s. doz.

tigrinum, the common Tiger Lily, with scarlet flowers, spotted maroon, and tinted orange. Three bulbs in a pot to form a clump for 9d. ; 12 pots, 8s.

tigrinum flore pleno, a perfect double Lily, flowers large and full, lasting in perfection longer than any other Lily: one of the last of this group to flower, colour similar to *Fortunei.* 6d.; 5s. doz.

tigrinum splendens, the grandest of the Tigers; black polished stems 6ft. in height, supporting a pyramid of fiery scarlet flowers spotted with crimson. 6d. ; 5s. doz.

Thomsonianum (*Lind.*) **roseum** (*Wallich*).   Distinct in character from any other Lily in cultivation ; a spike of 20 to 30 bright rose-coloured flowers, flowering in May. 1s. each.

Washingtonianum. This lovely Lily must not be omitted from any select list of Lilies, the flowers are pure white shading to lilac, and deepening with age to rose, and very sweet scented. Extra fine roots, 1s. 6d. and 2s. 6d. each.

Wallichianum superbum (sulphureum), a new species of great merit, distinct in every way from all others; hardy, very vigorous in habit, grows 5 to 8ft.; flowers tubular, 8 to 12ins. in length, of a pale yellow tinted with pink, and very fragrant. 3s. 6d. & 5s.

L. Monadelphum var. Szovitzianum
(see page 65).

Oriental Poppies.

I have for many years been devoting a great deal of attention to the improvement of this family, and have succeeded in raising a number of very beautiful varieties. A few years since they were scarcely known outside of a Botanic Garden, but now they are a feature at every Exhibition, and are being grown in great quantities by the Market growers for general decoration. For outdoor decoration there is nothing to equal them, their gorgeous crimson and scarlet flowers, and their immense size, render them conspicuous in any position, while the smaller growing varieties form fine subjects for massing, for borders, the rockery, and for cutting, for which purpose they are specially adapted. They are all perennial, quite hardy, very free growing, will thrive in any soil, and produce an abundance of most brilliant flowers.

Next season I hope to introduce a **New Seedling White Oriental Poppy**, the first ever offered.

Brilliant (*Ware*), a strong-growing variety with vivid vermilion flowers having large black blotches in the centre. The flowers resemble very much a huge *P. umbrosum*, but are much larger and more effective, a grand variety. Was awarded a First-class Certificate. 6d.; 5s. dz.

Papaver Royal Scarlet.

Bracteata (*true*), a charming species, producing numerous stout leafy stems, 2½ feet in height, with immense deep blood crimson flowers having a black blotch at the base of each petal, with conspicuous leafy bracts. 1s. ; 10s. 6d. doz. Seed, 6d. pkt.

Blush Queen (*Ware*), the flowers are large and of a pale blush pink, the base of the petals being blotched with deep purple. Was awarded a First-class Certificate by the Royal Horticultural Society. 9d. each ; 8s. doz.

Immaculata (*Ware*), a very distinct variety having bright orange-scarlet cup-shaped flowers, without the black blotch, which is so characteristic of this family. 9d. each ; 8s. doz.

Little Prince (*Ware*), miniature form, only growing 2 feet, with wiry stems, and small fiery-scarlet flowers produced in great profusion ; this will be eagerly sought after for cutting purposes on account of its colour, size and quantity of flowers produced. 1s. 6d.

Multiflora, this very distinct variety introduced from Central Europe has proved a very valuable acquisition, the small cup-shaped, blood-crimson flowers being highly appreciated for cutting purposes. 6d. each ; 5s. doz. Seed, 6d. packet.

Orientale (*The large Oriental Poppy*), a bold and very showy old-fashioned garden plant, producing, when well established, large quantities of crimson-scarlet flowers, usually with a black blotch which is so characteristic of this group. 6d.; 5s. doz. Seed, 3d. packet.

Orientale plenus (*Ware*), another great advance in the improvement of this family, being a really double form, the centre being well filled with long narrow filaments. The flowers are very large, of an orange-scarlet, and wonderfully free blooming, a first-class variety. 1s. 6d. each.

Pilosum, a distinct species, very dwarf, flowers brick-red, a most peculiar shade. 9d.; 7s. 6d. doz.

Prince of Orange (*Ware*), dwarf compact habit, producing an abundance of orange-scarlet flowers, quite a distinct shade. This variety was the great attraction at the great Botanic Exhibition, where it was awarded a First-class Certificate. 1s.; 10s. 6d. doz.

Royal Scarlet (*Ware*), is a strong growing variety, 3½ feet in height. The flowers are unequalled for size and brilliancy, when fully expanded, measuring 12 inches across, and of a glowing scarlet colour. One of the most remarkable varieties yet raised, and one of the grandest hardy perennials that can possibly be imagined. Was awarded First-class Certificate. 1s. each; 10s. 6d. doz. Seed, 6d. per packet.

Salmon Queen (*Ware*), quite a novel shade amongst Poppies, and I am sure will be much sought after on account of its colour which is a charming soft salmon scarlet. 1s. 6d. each; 15s. doz.

Semi-plena (*Ware*), this was very much admired in my collection of cut flowers at the Crystal Palace Show, and was honoured with a First-class Certificate. The flowers are of a glowing rich crimson, having two or more rows of petals, giving them the appearance of being double. 1s. each; 10s. 6d. doz. Seed, mixed colours, 6d. packet.

Six distinct varieties for 4s. 6d., 6s. and 8s. One of each of the above varieties for 10s.

Iceland Poppies (Papaver nudicaule).

No words of mine can convey any idea of the beauty of this charming group, and I am not in the least surprised at the enormous demand for both seeds and plants, their simplicity, elegance, and bold bright colours, commanding the attention of everyone, and the more they are known the more they will be appreciated. The figure given in my Seed Catalogue, will convey a good idea of the group, they grow about one foot in height, forming neat compact tufts of glaucous Fern-like foliage, surmounted by numerous flowers having a pleasant Lilac-perfume, continuing in bloom the whole of summer. For massing, the rockery, borders, or for cutting purposes, they are the most lovely in my collection.

Nudicaule (*Yellow Iceland Poppy*).—Very showy, clear yellow flowers. 6d.; 5s. doz. Seed, 6d. pkt.

Nudicaule alba (*White Iceland Poppy*).—Beautiful pure white flowers with golden-yellow anthers, forming a striking contrast, one of the best for cutting. 6d.; 5s. doz. Seed, 6d. pkt.

Nudicaule Miniatum (*Orange Iceland Poppy*).—Has brilliant orange-scarlet flowers. Awarded a First-Class Certificate by the Royal Horticultural Society. 6d.; 5s. doz. Seed, 6d. pkt.

Hepaticas.

A well known group of early Spring-flowering plants, forming tufts about nine inches in height, smothered with large red, blue, white, pink, and mauve, single and double flowers. They will thrive in any ordinary border, but do best when slightly shaded.

Acutiloba, a North American variety with pale blue flowers and large green leaves. 1/6; 15/- dz.

Angulosa, sky-blue flowers, as large as a half-crown; very distinct from the ordinary species, and one of the easiest to grow; without a doubt one of the very best of our Spring flowers: Strong clumps from ground, full of flower buds, 9d.; 8s. doz.

Triloba alba, white with red anthers, very conspicuous. 9d.; 8s. doz.

Triloba coerulea, deep blue, very free flowering. 6d. to 1s. 6d.; 5s. to 15s. doz.

Triloba coerulea fl. pl., double deep blue, a beautiful variety, and exceedingly rare. Small plants, 1s. 6d.

Triloba rubra, single deep red, free flowering and exceedingly showy. 6d. to 1/-; 5s. to 10/6 dz.

Triloba rubra fl. pl., very double well-formed flowers; bright and distinct. 6d. to 1s.; 5s. to 10s. dz.

Triloba variabilis, pretty marbled foliage, and large handsome flowers varying from lilac to blue or white, and changing colour with the season. Invariably flowering in autumn as well as spring. 9d.; 8s. doz.

Six distinct varieties, my selection, strong plants, for 3s. 6d.

Hardy Cyclamen.

A very interesting group of hardy bulbous plants. Some flower early in the Autumn, while others flower in spring. For pot culture in cold frames they are invaluable, and form, under good culture, magnificent specimens. For the rock garden, borders, naturalized in half-shaded places, in light vegetable soil, they form very attractive objects, and will soon form luxuriant masses, producing flowers of various shades in profusion. *Extract from* THE GARDEN :— "*Among the hardy flowers shown at the Royal Horticultural Society, none attracted so much attention as the little* CYCLAMEN ATKINSI, *of which there were several varieties and good sized specimens exhibited by* Mr. T. S. WARE."

Atkinsi roseum, marbled foliage with bright rose coloured flowers. 9d. ; 8s. doz.

Atkinsi purpureum, beautiful marbled foliage, bright purple flowers. 9d. ; 8s. doz.

Seedling varieties of the above mixed, in every shade of colour, 6d. each ; 5s. doz.

Africanum *(macrophyllum)*, immense foliage, large reddish-crimson flowers. 1s. ; 10s. dz.

europæum, this is the common Swiss Autumn-flowering Cyclamen, with bright rose-coloured flowers, very free blooming, and wonderfully effective. 6d. ; 5s. doz.

hederæfolium, this is the showiest species in this group, varying considerably in foliage and flower; the bulbs grow to a great size, forming masses of beautifully marbled foliage, and hundreds of flowers varying from bright rose to deep crimson. 6d. & 9d. ; 5s. and 8s. doz.

hederæfolium album, a variety of the preceding with white flowers, one of the most effective. 1s. ; 10s. doz.

Neapolitanum, delicate rose-coloured flowers, similar in habit to *C. Hederæfolium*, leaves distinctly zoned with white above, a very attractive variety. 9d. ; 8s. doz.

Cyclamen Hederæfolium.

repandum, a great beauty, forming masses of deep green leathery foliage, surmounted by innumerable deep reddish flowers early in spring. It is perfectly hardy, succeeding best in a light loam mixed with peat or leaf mould, partially shaded. 9d. ; 8s. doz.

vernum, very distinct variety, fine marbled foliage and bright rose-coloured flowers. 1s. ; 10s. doz.

vernum album, an exceedingly rare and beautiful variety, with snow-white sweet scented flowers, and marbled foliage ; very late in Spring. 1s. 6d.

6 distinct varieties, strong plants in pots, for 4s. and 6s.

Gaillardias.

For want of space I have been compelled to insert these in my Florist Flower Catalogue, to which refer for names and descriptions. This family is indispensable in every garden, either for decoration or for cutting ; flowers remarkably free, very large, and remarkably brilliant in colour. *For full description, see Catalogue No.* 144.

New Cannas.

A splendid collection of these will be found enumerated in my New Catalogue, No. 144, published with this edition. The full collection will appear in my Dahlia Catalogue, published in April, when the plants will be ready to plant out.

1. *H. punctatissimus.*   2. *H. maximus.*   3. *H. Apotheker Bogren.*

Helleborus, or Lenten Roses.

The two top flowers give a faithful portrait of this charming group of spring flowering plants, quite distinct from the "Christmas Rose" (the centre flower), which are evergreen and flower at Christmas, while these in most cases are deciduous and flower at "Lent," hence the name "*Lenten Roses.*" They are exceedingly varied in growth and in flower forming clumps of large coriaceous foliage, some attaining 2 feet in height, producing abundance of white, pink, red and purple flowers, many of them beautifully spotted and splashed. They are all of the easiest growth, perfectly hardy, preferring a good rich loam, in a somewhat shady situation or even planted between shrubs, and can be easily grown in pots.

atrorubens, this is one of the freest and most charming of this group, having long persistent foliage and beautiful bright purple flowers in March; one of the best.   2s. ; 21s. doz.

colchicus, a rare Caucasian species, very robust and beautiful; the leaves when young are deep purple; flowers rich purple; large and imbricated, flowering in early spring. 2s. 6d.; 24s. doz.

guttatus, a very beautiful variety, having large deep green leaves and large expanded flowers, pure white, clearly spotted with purplish-crimson. 2s. 6d.

guttatus var. sub-punctatus, a vigorous growing variety having large deep green leaves and white flowers, faintly spotted with purple; one of the best. 1s. 6d.; 15s. doz.

lividus (*corsicus*) (*trifolius*), a very distinct and handsome evergreen species, growing from 2 to 3 feet in height, with large coriaceous spiny leaves, a really handsome foliage plant. The flowers are small but numerous, of a bright green colour. 1s.; 10s. 6d. doz. Ex. strong, 1/6.

lividescens, another very rare species, with very large coriaceous foliage, but deciduous; flowers large and very globular, of a curious livid shade, and a very interesting plant. 2/6.

olympicus, a robust species having large globular and globular flowers, of a greenish white, produced in great abundance. 1s.; 10s. 6d. doz.

orientalis, dwarf, distinct habit, flowers greenish white, tinted with rosy-purple. 1s.; 10/6 dz.

orientalis Apotheker Bogren, a magnificent variety, having large globular flowers, of a deep crimson purple, veined and spotted deep crimson, one of the most beautiful of the new hybrid vars. 3s. 6d. *See* fig. 3, page 70.

orientalis Frau Irene Heinemann, flowers very large, fully expanded, beautiful rosy-purple colour, spotted with deep crimson, a very conspicuous variety. 3s. 6d.

orientalis Gretchen Heinemann, rosy-purple flowers, spotted crimson. 3s. 6d. each.

orientalis roseus, one of the best forms of "*orientalis*," the leaves larger, and more vigorous, and the flowers are of a beautiful rosy-purple colour and of great size. 1s. 6d.; 15s. doz.

orientalis purpureus, flowers deep purple, spotted and veined crimson. 1s. 6d.; 15s. doz.

orientalis viridescens, a very strong growing variety, with large deep green leaves and globular green, or greenish white flowers. 9d.; 8s. doz.

orientalis Willy Schmidt, large white flowers, exterior tinted green. 2s. 6d. each.

punctatissimus, one of the most vigorous of this group. The flowers are produced in great abundance, of a beautiful deep purplish crimson, spotted and veined deep crimson, the flower stalks and leaves in a young state are of a deep purple. *See* fig. 1, p. 70. 1/6; 15/- doz.

purpurascens, an interesting and handsome species with large deciduous foliage and globular "Dove" coloured flowers produced from January to March. 2s. 6d. each.

Twelve distinct varieties of Christmas and Lenten Roses for 12s., 18s. & 24s.

Helleborus, or Christmas Roses.

These are all varieties of *Helleborus Niger*, differing more or less in foliage, flower, time of flowering, &c., the whole flowering in succession from October to January, and forming an invaluable group for cutting purposes during the dead months of the year. They are best planted in spring for next season's display.

Will be supplied from the open during the planting season, afterwards sent in pots.

niger angustifolius (*St. Brigid's Christmas Rose*), a beautiful and scarce form, and one of the most distinct. The flowers are large and imbricated, and of the purest white. 1s.

major, one of the best, wonderfully free blooming, leaves long and leathery of a deep green, producing flowers from the middle of December till March, which are pure white and large. Small plants, 9d. each; 8s. doz. Stronger, 1s., 1s. 6d. to 3s. 6d. each, according to size.

maximus (*Altifolius*), the earliest and largest foliage, very large, often attaining 3ft. in height; large white flowers tinted with rose from October till January. *See* fig. 2, p. 70. 1s. 6d. each.

Madame Fourcade, has a neat, close habit, very dwarf, with coriaceous greenish-brown foliage, medium sized, pure white flowers from December till January. Nice plants, 1/6; 15/- doz.

niger (type), this is the old white variety, invaluable for cutting, very free blooming. 6d.; 4/- dz.

Riverstoni, a very distinct and meritorious variety, having undulated narrow leaves of a bright green colour, and large white flowers slightly tinted with rose and sweetly scented. 2s. 6d.

rubrus (*Apple Blossom*), large well formed flowers, white, tinged with rose, flowering from February till April. This should be in every garden. 1s. 6d. & 2s. 6d. each; 15s. & 24s. doz.

vernalis (*caucasicus*), of vigorous erect habit, large deep green persistent foliage, pure white flowers tinted rose on the exterior, and scented, flowering in great abundance until March. 2s.; 21s. doz.   One strong plant of each of the above 8 vars. for 10s. 6d. & 17s. 6d.

Hardy Terrestrial Orchids.

This is a very interesting and pretty group, containing some of the most beautiful hardy plants in cultivation. Some of the indigenous species are very pretty, and well worth growing; but bear no comparison to the still more beautiful Habenarias, Cypripediums, and other families, collected from other parts of the globe. Some of them are simply grand, their immense spikes, lively colours, and beautiful fresh foliage render them exceedingly effective, and in some cases are quite as beautiful as their tropical allies, which require heat to grow them in. No group of plants has more admirers than these, and everyone who has seen them growing well are struck with their exquisite loveliness and the gorgeous colouring of some of this family. I have several beds in a damp shady situation, filled to the depth of 20 inches with rough boggy peat, in which I grow a large number of this family, all of which grow luxuriantly, increasing in size and beauty every season. A large number of this family will grow in a situation similar to the one described, others require calcareous loam, which can be made by simply adding chalk, old mortar, &c., others like a little sun, but I have endeavoured to give sufficient instructions to enable anyone to cultivate them. All the Cypripediums and a great many other Orchids are also well adapted for pot culture, and will, with few exceptions, force well.

† Abundance of moisture in peat and loam in a shady situation, in fact might be treated as bog plants.

‡ Moist, at all seasons, peat, loam and leaf mould, in a well drained shady situation.

|| Planted in heavy calcareous soil, or clay mixed with pieces of limestone.

§ Good meadow loam, or leaf mould, half shady and moderately moist.

g Greenhouse.

NOTE.—*Orchids should be planted as early as possible, especially the Ophrys, Orchis, and Serapias.*

§ **Aplectrum hyemale**, a rare Orchid, closely allied to the *Lady's Slippers*, producing one large single leaf lasting through the winter, and racemes of pretty flowers, with brown perianth and white lip spotted with purple. 1s. 6d.

‡ **Bletia hyacinthina** (*Cymbidium*), a beautiful hardy Orchid from China, having narrow grass-like foliage, and terminal racemes of rosy-pink flowers; hitherto this has been considered a Greenhouse plant, but have seen it established in the open in many places, and I think it must be considered hardy. 1s. 6d. & 2s. 6d.

§ **Calopogon pulchellus**, next to the *Cypripedium* this is one of the most showy of hardy Orchids, the leaves are linear and grass-like, scape slender about a foot high, bearing in long terminal racemes several large flowers, sepals and petals of a beautiful pinkish purple, lip spreading and hinged bearded with white, yellow and purple hairs. A pan shown by me at the Royal Horticultural Society, attracted great attention, and was unanimously awarded a First-class Certificate. 1s. each; 10s. 6d. doz.

Cypripedium acaule.

|| **Cephalanthera pallens** (*Epipactis grandiflora*), next to *Cypripedium calceolus* this is the prettiest of British Orchids, flowers racemose, large white. 1s.; 10s. 6d. doz.

|| **Cephalanthera rubra**, flowers in long racemes, of a beautiful rosy-purple colour. 1s.; 10s. 6d. dz.

§ **Cypripedium acaule** (*Stemless Lady's Slipper*), a very handsome species, having a pair of large downy leaves and one or more very large blossoms; sepals and petals purple, lip much inflated of a pale rosy purple, one of the most beautiful. *See* fig. above. 1s. 6d. and 2s. 6d. each; 15s. and 24s. doz.

† **Cypripedium arietinum** (*Ram's Head Lady's Slipper*). A rare species seldom seen in cultivation, producing leafy stems supporting a solitary flower; the petals and sepals are brown, while the lip is veined with white and red. 2s.; 20s. doz.

‡ **Cypripedium candidum** (*White Lady's Slipper*), a very rare and beautiful North-American species, growing about a foot high, and bearing several flowers, sepals and petals white tinted purple, the labellum pure white. 2s. 6d. each.

‖ **Cypripedium calceolus** (*English Lady's Slipper*), one of the most beautiful of all our British plants, very free-flowering, vigorous in growth; flowers on stems about a foot in height, sepals and petals of a brownish purple, and the lip a bright golden-yellow and very fragrant. 1s. and 1s. 6d.; 10s. 6d. and 15s. doz.

† **Cypripedium parviflorum**, closely allied to *C. pubescens*, stems attaining a height of 18 inches, supporting one or more flowers, sepals and petals brown, labellum pale yellow and sweetly scented. 2s.; 21s. doz.

‡ **Cypripedium pubescens** (*Downy Lady's Slipper*), in growth resembling *C. calceolus* but the flowers are larger, the sepals and petals longer of a brownish purple, lip yellow. 1s. 6d. & 2s. 6d. each; 15s and 24s. doz.

Cypripedium calceolus.

† **Cypripedium spectabile** (*Showy Lady's Slipper*). The most beautiful of all the hardy Cypripediums, and there are but few among the tropical species to surpass it. It grows about 18 inches in height, bearing from one to three large flowers. The sepals and petals are large and rounded almost pure white, the lip much inflated is of a bright rose or pink colour. It is easily grown in any cool shady situation or grown in pots. I have here beds which have been for years one of the chief attractions in my Nursery every summer. Strong flowering plants, these will be at first supplied from the ground, later on in pots, 1s. 6d., 2s. 6d., 3s. 6d. each; 15s., 24s., 36s. doz.

‡ **Epipactis ensifolia**, long racemes of white flowers in late summer, very robust and free-flowering. 1s.

‡ **Epipactis palustris**, large white flowers tinted rose, a fine plant for a damp shady situation. 9d.; 7s. 6d.

‡ **Epipactis rubiginosa**, pretty reddish purple flowers, very vigorous and free. 9d.; 7s. 6d. doz.

‡ **Epipactis latifolia**, long racemes of white and purple flowers, and very easily grown. 9d.; 7s. 6d. doz.

§ **Goodyera Menziesi**, a pretty close growing evergreen plant with cordate glaucous green leaves beautifully marbled, and spikes of white flowers. Strong established plants, 1s. 6d. each.

Cypripedium spectabile.

‖ **Gymnadenia albida**, a rare British plant with dense spikes of small white flowers. 1s.

‖ **Gymnadenia conopsea** (*Gnat Orchis*), spikes of pretty bright rose-coloured flowers, agreeably perfumed; partial shade in loam and leaf mould. 9d.; 8s. doz.

‖ **Gymnadenia odoratissima** (*Sweet-scented Gnat Orchis*), a pretty free-flowering species, with fragrant pink flowers in close spikes. 9d.; 8s. doz.

‖ **Habenaria bifolia** (**Platanthera**) (*Common Butterfly Orchis*), spikes of pure white fls. 9d.

‡ **Habenaria blephariglottis** (*White-fringed Orchis*), one of the finest of this genus, with long spatulate leaves, and spikes of beautiful white flowers. 1s. 6d.; 15s. doz.

† **Habenaria ciliaris** (*Yellow-fringed Orchis*), the handsomest of this genus, very robust and vigorous in growth, very free flowering, leaves large ovate, stem from 18 inches to 2 feet in height, and bearing a long spike of large deep golden-yellow flowers, most beautifully fringed. The lip is large and spreading furnished with a beautiful hair-like fringe, so dense as to render it one of the most beautiful of this genus, fond of a very damp situation in peat or sphagum. 1s. 6d.; 15s. doz.

‖ **Habenaria chlorantha**, with large white flowers, very robust. 6d.; 5s. doz.

‖ **Habenaria fimbriata** (*Fringed Orchis*), without question one of the most beautiful of this family, and as easy to grow as an ordinary border plant. I have flowered it this season 2ft. high, with from 30 to 50 flowers upon a spike, varying in colour from rose to crimson, and lasting in bloom about three weeks; it flowers in June. 1s.; 10s. 6d. doz.

‖ **Habenaria dilatata**, one of the best of this genus with long spikes of pure white flowers, sweetly scented. 1s.; 10s. doz.

† **Habenaria psycoides**, one of the most beautiful, spikes of bright purple flowers on stems 18 inches in height, a grand plant for a very boggy situation. 1s.; 10s. 6d. doz.

‖ **Ophrys arachnites**, petals greenish purple, sepals rose, long brown lip. 9d.; 7s. 6d. doz.

‖ **Ophrys apifera** (*Bee Orchis*), pretty bronzy-pink flowers, one of the prettiest of the British species. 9d.; 7s. 6d. doz.

‖ **Ophrys aranifera** (*Spider Orchis*), large brownish flowers, very interesting. 9d.; 7s. 6d. doz.

‖ **Ophrys aurea** (**O. vespifera**) (*Wasp Orchis*), large golden yellow flowers, one of the finest of this group. 1s.; 10s. 6d. doz.

‖ **Ophrys aurea major**, taller and with larger flowers than the preceding. 1s.

‖ **Ophrys Bertoloni**, flowers large brownish-purple, rare and interesting. 1s.; 10s. 6d. doz.

‖ **Ophrys bombilifera** (*Humble-bee Orchis*), large handsome flowers, bright chocolate and rose spikes about 1 foot high; very pretty and distinct. 9d.; 8s. doz.

‖ **Ophrys Branciforti**, an elegant species with long racemes of deep rosy purple flowers, resembling a tropical *Epidendrum*; a fine plant for the rockwork or for pots. 9d.; 7s. 6d. dz.

‖ **Ophrys muscifera** (**Myodes**) (*Fly Orchis*), deep rich purple flowers, resembling a fly, a very vigorous growing and pretty species. 9d.; 7s. 6d. doz.

‖ **Ophrys scolopax**, flowers large and handsome, long oval lip tinted black, and sepals and petals brownish purple. 9d.; 7s. 6d. doz.

‖ **Ophrys tenthredinifera** (*Saw-fly Orchis*), a very pretty and robust species with large brownish flowers. 1s.; 9s. doz.

‖ **Ophrys speculum** (*Looking Glass Orchis*), perhaps the most interesting and handsome of this genus; flowers brown, tinted with blue, a remarkble combination. 1s.; 10s. doz.

‖ **Orchis anthropophora**, flowers purple, with small bright red lip and brown anthers. 9d.; 7/6 doz.

§ **Orchis foliosa** (*Leafy Orchis*), the grandest of this genus, and one of the easiest to grow, the leaves are broad about a foot long, gracefully recurved, the stem attains a height from 1 to 2 feet; the flowers are very numerous, disposed in large dense spikes, individual flowers rather large, of a beautiful deep purple. It is of vigorous growth, growing in almost any soil, provided it is not too heavy, and moderately damp during the growing season. Strong flowering plants, 2,6 and 3/6.

‖ **Orchis fragrans**, flowers small, in a dense spike, purple and white, very sweetly scented, a very rare and curious species. 9d.; 7/6 doz.

‖ **Orchis fusca** (*Brown Man Orchis*), bold handsome spikes 18 ins.; individual flowers large, white and brown, lip dark spotted; one of the showiest of the British species. 9d.; 8/- doz.

‖ **Orchis funera**, long spikes of deep sombre looking flowers. 9d.; 7/6 doz.

‖ **Orchis globosa**, large spherical heads of bright rose flowers; the flower spike is distinct in form from any other of this genus and very easily grown. 9d.; 8/- doz.

‖ **Orchis incarnata**, loose spikes of pale pink flowers, tinted purple. 9d.; 7/6 doz.

‖ **Orchis lactea**, flowers large, deep purple lip deeply divided. 9d.; 7/6 doz.

‡ **Orchis latifolia** (*The Large-leaved Orchis*), spikes 18 to 24ins:, thickly set with purplish-crimson spotted flowers; the foliage is large, forming most luxuriant specimens. 6d.; 5s. doz.

‖ **Orchis longicornis**, flowers handsome deep purple, with darker lip and long spurred; resembling much *O. Morio*. 9d.; 7/6 doz.

‡ **Orchis maculata** (*Hand Orchis*), flowers lilac and purple spotted, purple spotted foliage. 6d.; 5/- doz.

‡ **Orchis mascula**, with large foliage and bright purple flowers. 6d.; 5/- doz.

‡ **Orchis Morio**, very dwarf, with rosy purple flowers, labellum deep purple. 6d.; 5/- doz.

‖ **Orchis militaris** (*Soldier Orchis*), the flowers are red and grey with dark stripes; the spikes are a foot in length closely set with flowers; requires a little shade. 9d.; 8/- doz.

† **Orchis Mumbyana**, a very beautiful Algerian species, growing about 3 feet high, bearing long spikes of deep purple flowers. 2/6; 24/- doz.

‖ **Orchis pallens (sulphurea)**, flowers soft yellow on spikes 9 to 12 inches in height. 9d.; 8/- doz.

‖ **Orchis papilionacea** (*The Butterfly Orchis*), flowers rosy-purple. 9d.; 8/- doz.

‖ **Orchis provinciale**, showy spikes of pale yellow fls., foliage beautifully spotted. 9d.; 7/6 doz.

‖ **Orchis pauciflora**, a fine Italian species, growing 9 inches, flowers large, bright yellow. 1s.

‖ **Orchis Robertiana**, a vigorous-growing species, with spikes of rather large purple fls. 1/6.

‖ **Orchis saccata**, a very showy and interesting species, with large rose-coloured fls. 1/-; 9/- doz.

Orchis sambucina, large spikes of pale yellow, Elder scented flowers. 6d.; 5s. doz.

‖ **Orchis sicula**, a rare species with beautiful purplish-rose flowers. 9d.; 7s. 6d. doz.

‡ **Orchis spectabile**, a bold showy species, 1 foot in height, bearing spikes of bright pinkish-purple flowers, one of the most showy of this genus. 1s.; 10s. 6d. doz.

‖ **Orchis stabiana**, a beautiful Italian species, producing large spikes of rose flowers. 2s.

‖ **Orchis undulatifolia**, foliage large, beautifully undulated, flowers red, in long compact spikes, one of the most effective of this genus, well adapted for pot culture. 9d.; 8s. doz.

† **Orchis ustulata**, flowers in a dense spike, sepals and petals deep purple, lip white spotted purple. 9d.; 7s. 6d. doz.

§ **Satyrium carneum**, a pretty species, growing 18 to 24 ins., flowers are very large, varying in colour from white to rose; must be grown in a greenhouse. 1s. 6d.

‖ **Serapias longipetala**, flowers brown with a long coppery purple lip. 9d.; 7s. 6d. doz.

‖ **Serapias neglecta**, a very rare dark-flowered species, with a long broad crimson lip. 9d.; 8/- dz.

COLLECTIONS OF HARDY ORCHIDS.

For growing in wet boggy positions in peat or leaf mould, or for growing in an ordinary shady border in loam, mingled with chalk, limestone, &c., or for any ordinary border. Cypripediums will not be included in the lower priced collections.

When ordering these collections, state the position they are required for.

10 distinct showy vars., for either situation as described above for 6/-, 9/-, 12/-, 15-/ & 18/-

20 distinct showy vars., for either situation as described above for 12/-, 15/-, 18/-, 20/- & 25/-

Calla nana compacta,
THE MINIATURE LILY OF THE NILE.

A novelty of no mean merit, one possessing so many attractions that it will at once obtain admission to every good collection of plants in the kingdom. The old Calla is a well-known plant, scarcely a collection is to be found without it, while for market work it is grown by thousands. As a decorative plant for general decoration the old variety is somewhat tall, and the flowers for general work too large, while the New variety will do away with these objections. To describe it briefly I should call it a miniature form of the common Calla, flowers smaller, of the purest white, a plant in every way far more useful than the old one, both as a decorative plant and also for cutting. Nice plants in pots, 1s. 6d. each; 15s. doz.

Calla nana compacta.—From "Garden World."

Helianthus, or Perennial Sunflowers.

The Perennial Sunflowers are the most effective in the whole range of late Summer and Autumn flowering plants, indispensable for large borders, woodland walks, &c., and especially where cut flowers are wanted in quantity. They are all remarkably free-flowering, and you can scarcely find a situation or soil in which they will not succeed. For naturalizing, some kinds are specially adapted, especially *rigidus, lætiflorus,* and *maximus;* these should be planted in masses, where they would form sheets of golden-yellow flowers, worth walking a mile to see, and supply cut flowers by the barrow-load for Church decorations or large vases. The whole of this family succeed well in smoky districts.

Helianthus multiflorus plenus.

Hookerianus, a tall growing species with bright yellow flowers. 1s.

giganteus, stems 8 feet high, bearing bright yellow fls. in great abundance. 6d.

lævis (*Heliopsis*), *atrorubens* of previous catalogues. — A strong vigorous grower, at least 4 feet, flowers small, of a deep orange yellow, a very distinct shade. 9d.; 7s. 6d. doz.

lætiflorus, this plant has hitherto been offered under the name of "*H. rigidus semi-plenus,*" under which name it was Certificated by the R. H. S. It is an American species, similar in growth and foliage to *H. rigidus,* but with larger flowers of a rich dark-yellow colour, the disc also being yellow instead of purple as in *H. rigidus,* and semi-double. This is indispensable for late cutting, coming into bloom long after the other Sunflowers have finished, and when flowers are becoming valuable. 9d.; 8s. doz.

lætiflorus Woolley Dodd, another variety flowering later, with bright yellow flowers, nearly double. 1s.

multiflorus, this is the ordinary perennial Sunflower, a good useful plant, both for cutting and decoration, grows about 4 feet, flowers bright yellow. 9d.; 8s. doz.

multiflorus maximus (*The Great Perennial Sunflower*).—An enormous growing variety, 6 to 7 feet, producing immense golden single flowers, almost as large as the annual species. This should be grown in every garden where sufficient space could be found for it. *The Garden,* Sept. 1886, says :—" Here is a plant for the million. Certainly it ought to be in every garden where flower borders are, for it is in our opinion the most beautiful of all Sunflowers." 9d.; 8s. doz.

multiflorus plenus. This is the old double perennial Sunflower, now called "*Anemonæflora,*" and is one of the most useful Autumn perennials in cultivation—will grow anywhere and in any soil, forming masses 4 feet in height, and producing myriads of flowers, of a rich golden-yellow. 9d.; 8s. doz.

HELIANTHUS MULTIFLORUS, "BOUQUET D'OR."

HELIANTHUS MULTIFLORUS GRANDIPLENUS (SOLEIL D'OR).

HELIANTHUS—continued

multiflorus (Bouquet d'Or).—I am pleased at being able to offer another very beautiful variety of the old perennial Sunflower, one long lost to cultivation, which I had the pleasure of re-introducing in 1891. It is totally dintinct from all others, having a character peculiarly its own, and so distinct as to attract the attention of everyone. It is remarkably free blooming, in fact the flowers are so dense as to form a complete bouquet; every flower standing out boldly from the foliage, and of the richest golden-yellow imaginable. The flower in form approaches "*Grandiplenus*," but the petals are only half the width, and reminds one at first glance of some of the Chrysanthemums. To show its distinctive character I have had a plate prepared, showing the difference between this and *Soleil d'Or* (*see* fig. page 77). Was awarded a First-class Certificate at the International Horticultural Exhibition, Earl's Court, October 9th, 1892. 1s. 6d. each.

multiflorus grandiplenus (Soleil d'Or).—Columns have appeared in various Horticultural papers respecting the merits of this plant. It grows about 4 feet in height—composed of numerous rigid stems smothered with large golden-yellow flowers, and for cutting and general decoration one of the very finest plants in the whole of my collection. 9d.; 8s. doz.

orgyalis.—A late autumn perennial growing from 5 to 6 feet in height, having long graceful foliage, and numerous bright yellow flowers on short stalks. 1s.

rigidus (*Harpalium*).—One of the best, flowers very large, of a bright golden yellow, with a black disc, it grows about 3 feet in height, flowers very freely, and forms a very attractive object, requiring plenty of room as it grows very rapidly. 6d.; 5s. doz.

rigidus præcox.—A variety of *Helianthus rigidus*, about 3 feet in height, having large deep yellow flowers with a yellow centre, quite distinct from *H. rigidus*, and three weeks earlier in bloom. A very useful decorative plant, very free blooming and quite hardy. 6d.; 5s. doz.

strumosus, a tall species, flowers dark yellow, very pretty in the shrubbery border. 9d.; 8s. doz.

6 good distinct vars. my selection, for 4/- | 25 in 6 distinct vars. my selection, for 12/-
12 in 6 distinct vars. my selection, for 7/- | 50 in 6 distinct vars. my selection, for 21/-

Trillium (*Wood Lily*).

A highly ornamental and interesting group of American plants, containing some of the most useful and pretty of the early spring flowering perennials. They are tuberous rooted, 3 leaves in whorls; flowers in three divisions—either white, deep purple or white and red—and all flowering very early in spring. They are all admirably adapted for the border, the wild garden, and are grand for pots as they force well. They prefer a light soil in a shaded moist spot. A beautiful illustration of this appeared in my last Illustrated Catalogue.

Cernuum, with broad pointed leaves, and nodding pure white flowers. 1s. each.

Erectum "atropurpureum" (*Purple Wood Lily*), flowers very deep crimson-purple, one of the earliest of this genus, in bloom at the beginning of March. 9d. each; 7s. 6d. doz.

Erectum *var.* **album,** a variety of the above, but with cream-coloured flowers. 9d.; 7s. 6d. doz.

Erythrocarpum (*Painted Wood Lily*), a gem, flowers pure white, painted with purple spots at the base of each division; prefers a damp shady spot in peat or leaf mould. Good plants in pots, 1s. each.

Grandiflorum, too much cannot be said of this beautiful plant, it is simplicity itself—exquisitely beautiful, and so easy to cultivate that it has always been a mystery to me why it has not been more extensively grown. In the spring it is simply lovely, its large snow-white flowers two to three inches across, and large pleasing green foliage, attract the attention of every one. It is hardy, very free-blooming, and only requiring a damp shady corner in light peaty soil. 6d.; 5s. doz.

Nivale (*The Snowy Wood Lily*), small ovate leaves, spotted and marbled with purple and white flowers, growing about 9 ins., flowering in February, often through the snow. 9d.; 7/6 doz.

Ovatum, a very dwarf-growing species with white flowers, very early in Spring. 9d. each.

Recurvatum, deeply recurved purple flowers, and pretty marbled foliage. 1s.; 10s. 6d. each.

Sessile *var.* **Californicum** (*new*), a fine robust variety of *T. sessile*, from which it varies by its much larger purplish leaves and creamy-white flowers, growing 2 feet high; one of the best of this genus. Was awarded a F.C.C. by the R.H.S. Strong plants in pots, 1/-; 10/6 doz.

6 distinct varieties for 4s. | 12 in 6 distinct varieties for 7s. 6d.

Begonias.

The largest and most comprehensive Catalogue of Begonias ever published was issued by me in January, containing descriptions of all the best known varieties yet raised, and offered at prices far less than they have ever been offered before. The stock is immense and the collection unique, and I had the honor of being awarded the

FIRST PRIZE

at the great Begonia Contest last season, for one of the finest groups of Begonias ever seen at an Exhibition.

COPIES OF THE ABOVE CATALOGUE MAY STILL BE HAD.

Hemerocallis (Day Lily).

This is one of the most useful families we have, thoroughly hardy, true perennials, will last for 20 years without removing, and succeed in almost any soil or situation. They form bold handsome tufts of long, broad, radical leaves and clusters of Lily-like flowers of great substance, deliciously fragrant and exceedingly useful for cutting, and easily forced. Although the individual blossoms only last a day there is always a succession, so that no stem is without an expanded flower during the blooming season. All the buds will open in water, and the variegated forms make fine subjects for Exhibition purposes, and exceedingly useful for table decoration.

Disticha fl. pl., large broad foliage, at least 3ft. in height, from which issue stout stems, terminating with rich bronzy-yellow flowers. 9d.

Dumortieri, a gem for the border, for the rockery, or for cutting, only growing 2ft. in height, producing rigid stems bearing large numbers of flowers of a soft rich yellow, exterior bronzy-orange. 9d. each; 8s. doz.

Dumortieri præcox, similar to type, but quite a month earlier, a fine plant for cutting. 1s 6d.

flava, golden-yellow, very fragrant, fine for cutting and forcing, one of the very best hardy perennials in the whole of my collection. It is grand for cutting, most lovely when forced, and a plant that should be found in every garden, no matter how limited. 9d.; 8s. doz.

fulva, a bold handsome plant, 3ft. in height, with large and distinct fulvous flowers. 6d. & 9d.

graminifolia, a distinct species, flowers of a soft yellow colour, 1ft. high. 1s. each.

Kwanso fl. pl., large double flowers, of a rich bronzy-orange, a fine foliage plant. 9d. each.

Kwanso fl. pl. fol. var., handsome variegated foliage and double flowers, a fine plant for pots, adapted for almost any purpose, leaves are long and graceful, the variegation clear and distinct, rendering it exceedingly effective, it is quite hardy and a fine border plant. 2s. 6d.

Middendorfiana, a distinct species of a dark orange-yellow, growing 1ft. in height, very useful for cutting. Was awarded a First-class Certificate, June 14th, 1887. 1s. 6d. each

Thunbergi, bright yellow, 3ft. high, quite distinct from "*flava,*" being much later in bloom, and quite a distinct shade of yellow, very fragrant, a first-class border plant, very useful for cutting, as it blossoms long after all the other Day-Lilies have finished. 2s. 6d. each.

6 distinct vars., good strong plants, 4s. | 12 in 6 vars., 7s. 6d. ; extra strong, 10s. 6d.

Dahlias.

My Catalogue of these will appear in April, and will contain the best of each section, also a number of other plants adapted for summer decoration.

Phlox setacea.

Phlox setacea, Bride.

Alpine Phlox.

There are comparatively few persons who have any conception of the beauty of the different species of Phlox. The late flowering varieties of "decussata" and "suffruticosa" are recognized as indispensable for autumn decoration, but the spring flowering kinds are scarcely known. Every variety here mentioned is well worth growing, as they produce an abundance of flowers and increase rapidly. Most of them are evergreen, and all are perfectly hardy and invaluable for spring bedding, edging, the rockery, or for borders.

For autumn flowering vars. of Phlox Decussata and Suffruticosa, see my *Florist Flower Cat.*

Amœna, the most beautiful of this lovely group, somewhat robust in habit, producing large clusters of bloom of the most perfect circular outline, combined with its brilliant lovely pink colour. One of the finest plants for spring massing in cultivation. 9d. each; 8s. doz.

Canadensis, a slender growing species, about 1 foot in height, with numerous stems supporting corymbs of pale blue flowers in spring. 9d.

Canadensis alba (*new*), similar to preceding but far more vigorous in constitution, with flowers pure white, which forms a lively contrast to its bright green foliage. 1/-; 10/- doz.

Caroliniana var. ovata, a strong growing variety, producing corymbs of large bright purplish-red flowers in late spring; one of the best border perennials in cultivation. 1s.

Nelsoni, cushions of evergreen moss-like foliage, spangled with white flowers in spring. 6d.

Procumbens, one of the most distinct of the Alpine section, forming creeping tufts of small purplish-green foliage, with clusters of lilac-coloured flowers with violet centres; exceedingly free blooming, and one of the most effective for spring bedding. 6d.

Setacea varieties, these form a group of dwarf, compact masses of evergreen foliage, covered in early spring with bright lively coloured blossoms, varying from white to bright rose; all are quite hardy, very free growing; charming for the rockery, borders, lines, massing, &c.

Setacea atropurpurea, one of the most vigorous of the group, forming large masses of foliage, which is thickly studded with purplish-rose coloured flowers, with a crimson belt. 6d.

Setacea Bride, neat dwarf compact habit, flowers very numerous, pure white with a red centre; very conspicuous. 9d.

Setacea grandiflora, one of the best, neat dwarf habit, flowers large, very abundant, of a rich mauve, very distinct, and exceedingly free flowering. 9d.

Setacea Vivid, one of the most effective of the group, and one of the finest spring flowers in cultivation; the flowers are not so large as some, but far more abundant, of a bright fiery rose color, with a rich carmine centre. Was awarded a First-class Certificate. 1s.

Stellaria, a newly introduced species, having large flowers of a pleasing lilac color; one of the prettiest of the family. 9d.

Verna, heads of deep red flowers early in spring. 6d.

Calochortus, or Californian Tulips.

This group is as brilliant and as varied in colour as the Tulips, to which they are closely allied. They are (with a few exceptions) natives of California, consequently like abundance of sun heat, and a warm situation in light sandy soil; they would succeed at the base of a south wall, or on a sunny slope of the rockery, or can be grown in pots. The plants are established in pots, and should be planted at once, taking care not disturb the roots more than is really necessary. I would recommend planting them in groups three to six together, they seem to do better when thus planted, and are certainly far more effective than when planted singly. There are a great many varieties, all of which are worth cultivating, but I think the following are the best and most distinct.

Benthami, of very dwarf growth, flowers erect, golden yellow, marked with three conspicuous brown blotches, and densely covered with yellow hairs. 8d. each ; 6s. doz.

Gunnesoni (*C. Leichlini*), large flowers, of a delicate white, tinted with lilac at the base, and a purple band or spot above the base. 9d. each ; 7s. 6d. doz.

Lilacinus, leaves long and broad, flowers large and erect, pale lilac, on stems 9 inches high. 6d. each ; 5s. doz.

Luteus, an elegant species, numerous large yellow flowers, with three purple spots at the base, on branching bulbiferous stems about a foot high. 6d. each ; 5s. doz.

Macrocarpus, large glaucous foliage, and large deep lilac flowers on stout stems about 18 ins. high ; a very robust grower. Received a First Class Certificate. 9d. each ; 7s. 6d. per doz.

Maweanus, about 9 inches high, much branched ; flowers purplish-blue densely covered with long whitish hairs. 6d. each ; 5s. doz.

Nuttallii, flowers large, pale lilac or white, the tips of petals tinted with greenish-yellow, spotted purple or yellow. 9d. each ; 7s. 6d. per doz.

Pulchellus (*Cyclobotra*), flowers large, drooping, globular, with the segments overlapping of a deep golden yellow colour, and furnished with yellow hairs. One of the most distinct and beautiful of this genus, and the freest to grow. 6d. each ; 5s. doz.

Splendens, flowers large, of a clear lilac colour, lined with purple, and densely covered with white or pale lilac hairs, very elegant, and of free and robust habit. 6d. each ; 5s. doz.

Venustus var. oculatus, very showy ; the flowers are large, of a pale yellow colour, with a large central brown spot, bordered with yellow. Resembling at first sight a beautiful *Phalænopsis*. 9d. each ; 7s. 6d. per doz.

Venustus purpurascens, flowers large, much expanded, of a deep lilac purple, tinted with rose, and a large brownish spot at the base or centre of each of the segments. 6d. each ; 5s. doz.

Venustus var. roseus, flowers large, much expanded, of a light purple or white colour, tinted rosy purple, and two large deep rose blotches on each of the segments. One of the most showy of this genus. 9d. each ; 7s. 6d. doz.

Weedii, of recent introduction, closely allied to *C. venustus*, but much taller, and of a more vigorous and branching habit ; flowers large, deep yellow, edged brownish-purple, and covered densely with purple or golden yellow hairs. 1s. each ; 10s. 6d. doz.

12 in 12 varieties of the above for 5s.

Sarracenia purpurea.

Sarracenias & Carnivorous Plants.

This group contains some of the most remarkable in the Vegetable Kingdom—some only remarkable for their strange carnivorous habits, while others form beautiful subjects either grown in pots or in the open·air. All the Sarracenias are very beautiful, and all more or less hardy; some, such as *purpurea*, forming immense masses of pitcher-like leaves and still stranger flowers. They all require abundance of moisture; in fact, they are best described as bog plants, growing in any ordinary spongy soil—peat, perhaps, suiting them best.

Sarracenia Drummondi, an evergreen species growing from 1½ to 2ft. high; the leaves or pitchers are erect, light green in colour, while the apex and hood are beautifully variegated, white, red, and green; flowers large, of a crimson purple. This requires a cold frame or in a Fernery. 2s. 6d.

Sarracenia flava, stems about 2ft., having at the apex a large open throat, with a broad lid; the plant is of a pale yellowish green with yellow flowers. Small plants, 1/6; ex. strong 2/6

Sarracenia psittacina, an elegant species, very pretty and distinct, its small pitchers having a curiously curved lid or apex, of a rich purple and crimson, handsomely mottled with white. 2s. 6d.

Sarracenia purpurea, a prostrate species, having broad winged pitchers, the throat and lid very hairy, and beautifully veined and striped crimson. It is perfectly hardy, requiring abundance of moisture, and can be planted in either sun or shade, on the margin of a stream, or in a swamp; if planted in sun the color is far more intense than in the shade, but wherever planted it must have abundance of moisture, and planted in very spongy soil. 1s. 6d. & 2s. 6d.

Dionæa muscipula (*Venus's Fly Trap*), a curious plant, allied to the *Drosera*, having a number of prostrate leaves furnished at the edge with a thick row of bristle-like hairs; while in the centre of each are 3 short hairs which, when touched, cause the leaf to fold up, entrapping the insect, which soon dies; when this takes place the leaf again assumes its normal position. 2s. 6d.

Asters (*Michaelmas Daisies.*)

This little known group of plants has been steadily rising in popularity for some years past, and as the demand increased so, fresh exertions were made in finding new varieties to fill the demand, resulting in the accumulation of an immense collection, some of no value, while others were quite new to commerce, and in some cases far more beautiful than anything seen before. These were collected from all parts of the world, and when got together a great confusion existed with regard to their nomenclature, resulting in the Aster Conference by the "Royal Horticultural Society" at Chiswick, to determine their correct names, and to be able to select the best and most distinct out of the hundreds which were obtained by them from many sources.

Now the following list is a first-class selection, including all the good old ones and the best of the new ones, with the "Conference Names" they will in future be known by.

Acris, neat bushy habit, 2 feet in height, smothered with lilac-purple starry flowers. 9d.

Amellus Bessarabicus, one of the finest of this group, very early in bloom, producing large purplish-blue flowers with orange centres, 2 feet in height. 9d.

Corymbosa (*Biotia*), a grand variety for any position, having large cordate leaves deeply toothed at the base, having blackish-purple stems 3 feet in height, bearing large corymbose heads of starry white flowers with yellow centres, forming a very attractive object. Strong plants, 1s.

Diffusus horizontalis, numerous branching stems, smothered with red and white flowers, 2ft. high; very symmetrical in growth, and exceedingly effective. 9d.

Aster Novæ Angliæ rosea.

ASTERS—*continued.*

Ericoides, very distinct, long graceful sprays, completely covered with small white flowers. 1s.

Grandiflorus (*true*), the largest of all Asters, very scarce.   Plants ready in April, 2s. 6d. each.

Linosyris (*Goldilocks*), neat in habit, growing about 2 feet in height, bearing heads of bright yellow flowers. 9d.

Longifolius var. formosus (**Madame Soyneuce**), symmetrical bushes, 2 feet in height, covered with bright rose coloured flowers. 9d.

Multiflorus, branching sprays of small pure white flowers, very distinct. 9d.

Novæ Angliæ melpomene, very large bluish-purple flowers, with orange centres. 9d.

Novæ Angliæ rosea, clear rose-coloured flowers on stems 4 feet high ; distinct. 9d.

Novæ Angliæ rubra, bright rich crimson flowers, forming a pleasing contrast. 1s.

Novæ Angliæ, William Bowman (*new*), flowers slightly incurved, of a deep violet-purple, without doubt the finest of this section. 1s.

Novi Belgii, Archer Hind, erect habit, forming compact heads of soft blue flowers. 1s. 6d.

Novi Belgii decorus, heads of lilac flowers, 3 feet in height, very showy. 9d.

Novi Belgii densus, another fine variety, 4 feet high, bearing heads of pale blue flowers. 9d.

Novi Belgii formosissimus, very distinct heads of deep rosy lilac flowers on stems 4 feet high. 9d.

Novi Belgii, Harper Crewe, stems 3 feet high, bearing heads of large pure white flowers with yellow centres. 1s.

Novi Belgii, Lady Trevelyan, another fine variety with large pure white flowers, 3ft. high. 1s.

Novi Belgii Pluto, heads of bright blue flowers on stems 3 feet high. 9d.

Novi Belgii Purity, one of the best, producing large pure white flowers on stems 4ft. high. 1s.

Novi Belgii, Robert Parker, large sprays of beautiful lavender-blue flowers with yellow centres, extra fine. 9d.

Novi Belgii Versicolor, flowers of medium size, of every shade of colour from pure white to deep rose, on the same plant. 9d.

Polyphyllus, medium sized white flowers, very abundant bloomer. 9d.

Ptarmicoides, neat bushy habit, smothered with pure white flowers in August. 1s.

Turbinellus, long slender sprays with large lavender flowers, very fine. 1s.

Vimineus, very graceful in habit, long slender sprays of pure white flowers about 2½ft. high. 1s.

The above set of 26 varieties, excluding Grandiflorus, for 18s.

Many other varieties not enumerated here can be supplied, names upon application.

6 varieties for 3s. 6d. ; 12 varieties for 6s.

Culinary Roots, Herbs, &c.

RHUBARB.—A fine collection of all the leading kinds including JOHNSTON, ST. MARTIN, PRINCE ALBERT, PARAGON, STOTTS MONARCH, VICTORIA, RUBY, and others.

Strong roots 9/- doz., extra strong 12/- doz.

SEAKALE.—First size sold out for this season. II size for planting, 7/- per 100.

Artichoke, Globe } *price on*	Horse-radish	Sorrel, thick-leaved
,, Jerusalem } *application*	Lavender	Southernwood
Balm	Mint	Tarragon, 6d. each, 4s. 6d. dz.
Chives	Myrrh, sweet-scented	Thyme, common
Hop	Penny Royal	,, lemon
Horehound	Rue	,, lemon coloured
	Sage, Common	Wormwood

HERBS.—My selection, 3/- to 4/- per doz., in variety.

INDEX.

For any family not enumerated above, see my Florist Flower, Pæony, Fern, or Begonia Cat.

COREOPSIS GRANDIFLORA. *See* page 22.

R. E. Taylor & Son, Horticultural Printers, 19, Old Street, London, E.C.

European Nursery Catalogues
A virtual collection project by:
Bücherei des Deutschen Gartenbaues e.V.
Paper version of this catalogue hold by:
Bücherei des Deutschen Gartenbaues e.V.
Digital version sponsored by:
C.A.Wimmer